Mr. and Mrs. Smith's
Employment Survival Guide
(Business Edition)

By Mr. and Mrs. Smith

AuthorHouse™
1663 Liberty Drive
Bloomington, IN 47403
www.authorhouse.com
Phone: 1-800-839-8640

First published by AuthorHouse 2/25/2010

ISBN: 978-1-4490-6423-5 (e)
ISBN: 978-1-4490-6422-8 (sc)

Printed in the United States of America
Bloomington, Indiana

This book is printed on acid-free paper.

Dedication:

This book and every book that we are blessed to share with others are instantly dedicated to our Heavenly God. Our prayer, *"Lord please communicate thru us so that we can enlighten every reader that you are the only one that can relieve us from our financial decline and from all of our troubles".*

To:
Our mothers: Missionary Mildred Smith & Charlene Parker
Our fathers: Minister O. Smith & Walter Parker
Our sisters: Sherita, Mercheryl, Juanita, Carolyn & Kim
Our courteous and respectful children: Lil' O' & Aubrey

We love you all.
-Odie & Val

For unto whomsoever much is given, of him shall be much required:
Luke 12:48 (KJV)

Our Purpose:

The mission and contents of this book is to inform everyone of the effectiveness of enhancing their employment status. By exploring the available information and assistance presented, we believe that our eighteen years of experience in employment communication will be a rewarding presentation. We are blessed to assemble and present our knowledge of the employment field to you, because each page was written with you in mind.

-Mr. and Mrs. Smith

INTRODUCTION:

During our twenty-five years of working multiple jobs, we had always continued to improve our status on each job because we (like most employees) wanted to be a recognized employee who was the trusted and dependable *go-to* person. While on those jobs, we also tried to blend in to as many appropriate cliques as possible, but, as we discovered, this strategy did not guarantee nor protect our employment. When an employer decides that your time at their company is nonessential (through a layoff or termination), you may feel betrayed, as many of us would. We realized that every employee, regardless if they are a dedicated worker or not, is expendable. Both Mrs. Smith and I have lost many jobs during our careers, from layoffs due to staff downsizing, to the ill-famed statement; *"We are sorry, but your services are no longer needed."* Either way, being unemployed creates an anxiety and concern regarding your family's financial needs; and there is no easy way to receive a pink slip or accept the fact that you are about to lose your job. With our changing economy, it is difficult to know if our jobs are truly secure or if we are in safe hands with our employer. We are all replaceable.

This book will provide you with some assistance during your employment transition with what we call the O-D-I-E method:
- **O**rganizing yourself before leaving a job
- **D**eveloping a *To-Do* list after you have been released
- **I**mproving your chances during your search for another job
- **E**xecuting an appropriate work ethic while on your new job

We have collected a great deal of experience in the field of employment pursuit, and we would like to share our familiarity of unemployment compensation and survival suggestions.
-Mr. and Mrs. Smith

Contents

Education:

Résumés:

Interviews:

Working:

CHAPTER 1

How Do You Prepare to Leave Your Current Job?

Let's first define the terms *layoff* and *termination* and how you should handle each situation.

Layoffs: Most employees may have some idea whether their employer is prospering enough to sustain revenue and maintain their current staffing level. If the company is not profitable enough to continue business, then layoffs may be forthcoming. With many companies, layoffs are usually announced before they take place; but then there are employers who do not broadcast their business dealings with the employees, and layoffs may occur unexpectedly. Although many companies participate in employee placement programs, there are other resources that provide payment and employee advantages that every laid-off employee should be aware of—such as the Unemployment Compensation program. This program was designed to be an advantage to out-of-work employees and to pay compensation to those who are eligible. Although the weekly benefits do not entirely replace your paycheck, they can help you meet your expenses during your time off. We encourage unemployed workers to immediately file a claim for unemployment compensation. Even though a laid-off worker is entitled to receive future paychecks from their employer; he would benefit by filing a claim as soon as possible, because the first week he is unemployed is considered the verification or "holding" week.

Following my first layoff, Mrs. Smith and I did not understand the procedures for filing a claim, and we had to return to the Division of Unemployment Security many times to prepare and submit all of our personal documentation. Today, a claimant can file on the Internet, and only have to visit the unemployment office once a month. The online method will save you time and fuel.

Termination: There is no plan for being terminated, but you can prepare for the inevitable. Most employees can sense if there is a problem between them and their employer. An employer may offer the employee a voluntary resignation, thereby making the transition a mutual agreement. Being fired is the opposite of being laid off, because it is usually brought on by a dishonorable action of the employee. Although it may be embarrassing, it is not the end of the world. Under certain conditions, an employee who is fired might be eligible for unemployment compensation—but usually the worker will not receive severance pay, benefits, earned bonuses, or commissions. If the worker is entitled to unemployment compensation, it would be beneficial to file for unemployment during the same week of the termination. By filing the claim as early as possible, the unemployed worker can begin to collect unemployment compensation sooner.

As a young man, I was terminated from a job because of poor attendance, but since my termination was not considered "deliberate disloyal performance," I was able to collect unemployment compensation. At the time, I was not married and had no children, but it was still difficult to no longer receive that steady paycheck that I was accustomed to. It was my fault for being terminated, and I vowed to never take another job for granted. This incident was twenty-five years ago, and I have been blessed to have never experienced another termination.

Before you part ways with your employer, be sure to have an exit strategy and potential reentry employment plan. Prior to that, it would be to your advantage to:
- Take your personal property home. On your last day at work, the company may question whether an item belongs to you or to the company.
- Delete any personal e-mail or software from the company computer.
- Gather all of your updated contact information from your workstation and keep it for future exchange with prospective associates, clients, and acquaintances.
- Acquire letters of recommendation from your coworkers.

CHAPTER 2

Helpful Tips for Surviving a Layoff

Circumstances can vary—there are many distinctive survival situations and behaviors for anyone who has become a victim of downsizing: from a single young worker, who has the options to continue their education and find a part-time position to fulfill their lesser needs, to the laid-off parent, who must continue to provide for their family. Regardless, both of them are without a steady paycheck and will need assistance and encouragement. No job is 100 percent secure or guaranteed, and anyone is susceptible to a layoff. Here are a few suggestions on how you can conduct yourself:

Saying goodbye to your managers and coworkers: On the day of your layoff, if at all possible, cordially greet everyone you have either worked for or worked with. Exchange contact information so you can keep in touch for personal and employment updates. Staying in contact with former employers can be a useful networking tool for future employment.

Informing your Family: A layoff affects everyone within your household, either emotionally or financially. Your family members are the backbone of your support, but self-discipline and determination to endure this setback is your responsibility. This transition is best dealt with in the company of your family. Explaining your job loss to your children may be the most difficult part. Older children especially can imagine the worst: not having the money to pay for the mortgage, car payments or utilities. When informing your loved ones of your job loss, be totally honest with them by explaining the company's decision to downsize, and advise them that the family will have to cut back on some expenses. When you need a shoulder to lean on, turn to a loved one.

It's all right to be emotional: When the reality of it all sets in and your emotions appear, welcome them with self-control and managed composure. After facing the reality of being unemployed and having had time to collect your thoughts, your time to begin addressing the issue will soon follow. Although it may be very difficult to do, try to accept your layoff professionally and not take it personally. You might come to the conclusion that this could be a great opportunity to begin a new career. There are many emotional stages that you may encounter, such as: disbelief, anger, resentment and confusion.

Try not to become frustrated because there are no employers calling you: With our decelerated economy, even the search for an average-paying position may become difficult. There are college students who cannot obtain a job at a grocery store or fast-food restaurant because middle-aged parents are now being considered for these positions. Looking for a new job can be challenging and frustrating, but don't give up; there are employers who are seeking a persistent employee such as you.

Do not neglect yourself: Continue to care for your appearance and health, because when that employer does call you in for an interview, you want to appear pristine and flawless, as though it was your first day on the job. Look and feel positive. Continue to stay optimistic, motivated, and active. Staying confident and hopeful can increase your desire to achieve. Keep active by attending employment seminars, performing research at your local public library, staying in touch with other coworkers who were also laid off, and visit your unemployment office to explore available job openings.

Keep your résumé current: Your résumé is your bibliography, and when a potential employer examines it, you want it to tell them who you are, what you know, and where you would like to go. Your résumé is your introduction to a potential employer, and the first meeting should be a memorable one.

Stay focused and positive: There are many people who find it difficult to stay confident and motivated while seeking employment. One solution would be to imagine that you are receiving great pay for working the job of your dreams—but you only receive a great paycheck if you can find the next job of your dreams. Continue to search every available resource—career fairs, employment agencies, and career blogs—whatever you need to do to find that job. With this attitude and motivation, you are more likely to be successful in your search.

CHAPTER 3

Focus and Motivation

When you receive word that you will be laid off or terminated, it is one of the worse feelings that you will encounter, but there are actions that are acceptable and reactions that should never be displayed. Using profanity and exhibiting an offensive attitude will *burn the bridge* of retuning to work for this employer, (if you were recalled to come back to work for them). This is not the way you want to contribute on building a positive future career plan. We had encountered a few employees who had told their now former supervisor a few choice words, of which each of the employees did later regret. As corporation profits decline, thousands of people are losing their jobs everyday, and according to the evening news, there is no recovery in sight. There are many companies that provide certain employees an advanced two week notice (or more) of their layoff date. This can have a tremendous effect on your work ethic, mind, stress level and health, especially when the inescapable date approaches. It is a difficult struggle to prepare for unemployment and many employees may not be equipped with the clear direction that the employer should take. While on the job and as grief settles in, there are several ways that can help you with rational thinking and organizing your workday, such as:

Prioritize and organize your job duties:
Make a list at the start of your work day of what you will need to accomplish for the day and rank the activities by level of urgency. The more you are able to include all of the work assignments and your personal life into your priority routine, the more resourceful you will be able to perform. This is beneficial for everyone, regardless of their employment status.

Balance your schedule:
Try not to overload yourself with work duties, family life or personal conflicts. It is hard enough when you have to focus on your personal matters, but what can help is if you set weekly and daily goals for yourself. When you don't balance your schedule, you will go around in circles and you will not accomplish very much. The more balanced you are, the better your chances are of succeeding.

Time management:

A person who uses an effective time management strategy can be a very successful person. One way to accomplish this is by spending time in order to save time, and what we mean by this is, if you left home early enough to arrive to work everyday at least 10-15 minutes early, you will give yourself time to organize and command your day. Use your free time wisely by being productive and creative and you will discover that while on the job, you will be a very valuable employee and a key part of keeping your employer (and possibly your future employer, again) in business. At the same time, you will begin feeling more confident about yourself. Mr. Smith and I have encountered coworkers who were given 14-30 day layoff notices which stated "*due to budget constraints, the company regrets to inform you of the following layoffs*". This was devastating news to some of them, but it was an expected report for the others. Not only were each of them slightly embarrassed, because they had to continue working everyday while being viewed as a condemned employee, but each of them took the downsizing news differently. Some of the comments spoken from the soon to be laid off coworkers, which were heard around the workplace were: "I'm not going to work too hard, what are they going to do to me, lay me off early?", "I'm glad that I'm getting laid off, because I need the vacation" and "the company can't survive without me, I'm too valuable". To this day, we have never encountered an employer who withdrew the layoff notices because an employee was "too valuable". We are being direct when we say that when layoff notices are made public within a company, it is usually an unavoidable situation. Through the years, we have gained knowledge of the best ways to utilize your time wisely while unemployed or during a layoff notice and each of the details that we provide are very useful, such as:

- Deciding on **Which Bills Should You Pay First** (see Chapter 4)
- Discovering the best **Ways to Save Money While Unemployed** (see Chapter 5)
- Filing for state **Unemployment Insurance and Benefits** (see Chapter 6)
- Learning about **Tips for Applying for Unemployment** (see Chapter 7)
- Becoming skilled at **How to Write a Successful Résumé** (see Chapter 17)
- Researching and reviewing valuable **Interviewing Etiquette** (see Chapter 20)
- Studying quality **Interviewing Questions and Answers** (see Chapter 21)

Stressing Out:
Both Mr. Smith and I have experienced stress and pressure during our layoffs, and together, the first action we always perform was to pray and thank God that he has blessed us with a home, our two healthy children and for giving us a mind to survive by immediately seeking employment. Many employers today are equipped with a Human Resources manager who can provide workforce adjustment assistance, but there are lots of other employers who do not have the luxury of employing a Human Resources department. This can be very tense and stressful, especially if you do not have someone who can counsel and direct you in the proper direction. While some indications of tension from constant worry may be obvious to yourself and to others, there are many other warning signs that you may not notice, but others will. It would be in your favor to ask a loved one to be attentive and alert you if they witness any of the following stressful symptoms.

- Fatigue
- Headaches
- Muscle tension
- Social withdrawal
- Problems sleeping
- Stomach problems
- Trouble concentrating
- Using alcohol or drugs
- Loss of interest to work
- Feeling irritable or depressed
- Displaying loss of enthusiasm

During our layoffs, we will admit that our stress levels were approaching the alarming stages. Our family Doctor was very supportive with providing advice and valuable information on controlling any depression, anxiety or stress. His advice to us was:

Exercise regularly
This gives your body the natural boost. During the warmer days, we would walk several days each week in our neighborhood, and later, we purchased a tread mill to use during the colder days.

Regularly turn off the television and radio
This was incredible advice, because the TV can be a distracting device that will supply you with a daily dose of negativity, such as: crime, disasters, depressing gossip or unconstructive shows. We did not want to deal with any more negative information.

Take necessary breaks throughout the day
We learned how to relax ourselves when any of the symptoms materialized. One method that I utilized often was soothing long warm baths. This was my peaceful therapy.

Diet properly
When we learned to eat well, while exercising, we were able to get a good night sleep and begin every morning with a fresh outlook.

CHAPTER 4

Which Bills Should You Pay First?

Sometimes your budget is so stretched that creditors may be calling you on a daily basis. Everyone who has established credit has a credit rating, and it is important to protect that score. Without a steady paycheck, it is difficult to have a payment plan. There are several credit counseling services that can evaluate your budget and offer debt-management and financial advice for little or no cost. If you lose your job, you should immediately contact all of your creditors with this information. If you are a loyal customer who consistently pays their bill on time, each of the companies may place you on a benevolent plan of assistance by waiving late fees or allowing deferred payments. Following is the suggested priority order of paying your bills:

Family necessities: The obligations most important to your family are food, clothes and medical. When you have a limited supply of money, these are the essential elements that will help you sustain a healthy family. If you don't provide your family, who else will?

Mortgage/Rent: This should be your next priority, and everything else should circle around your home. If you are a homeowner, a house may be the largest investment that you will ever possess—and the most visible item on your credit score. Prior to one of Mr. Smith's layoffs in the nineties, the company had announced that layoffs could occur in the near future. However, the layoffs did not happen until one and one-half years later. Meanwhile, Mr. Smith began setting aside $75.00 per week from his paycheck prior to the layoff. He saved enough extra money to pay the mortgage for thirteen months. For an entire year, we did not have to worry about losing the house through foreclosure.

Utilities: Having any of your utility services interrupted could result in a reconnection fee. If you are laid off in the summer or winter months, the temperature could become unbearable to survive in your home. We believe that your utilities are the second most important bills to pay, especially if there is someone in the household who relies on a life-support machine, an infant who needs warm baby bottles, or any energy-dependant device that is absolutely necessary. A word of forewarning; the utility companies must notify you before they terminate your services so when you do receive a notice, it would be wise to inform them of your employment and financial status, because they may grant you a payment extension period. This extension may be an adequate amount of time for you to assemble enough money to pay on your bill.

Auto loans: You will need transportation to interviews, employment agencies, and meeting with potential employers. If your loan payment is preventing you from paying your other bills, you might consider using inexpensive public transportation, if available. Late payments are very visible on your credit report. During one of our layoff periods, we were low on funds and could not afford to pay our car note. Our auto loan company sympathized with us during the first month, and they offered to defer the late payment to the end of the loan contract; but if we had fallen three months behind on our payments, we were informed that our vehicle would have been repossessed.

Credit cards: Defaulting on credit card payments is very harmful to your future credit scores. If the account reaches a debt-collection agency, the agency may be commissioned to demand a payment, or the entire balance. Usually, if you have a high credit score, an agency may settle for a percentage of your balance, because they understand that you want to keep your high credit score. You may be more willing to preserve your credit rating and arrange a settlement. Following one of Mr. Smith's layoffs, we cashed in our Gold Card for cash advancement with our bank. Although we were truly struggling for money, it may have been the worst decision we ever made. Not only were we unable to repay our bank for the cash advancement, but our bank disclaimed us as loyal customers and our loan was sent to a collection agency. To this day, our combined credit score is still affected by the collection debt.

Income Taxes: There are many people who may feel that income taxes should be higher up on this list, but the theme while unemployed is all about survival. We are not suggesting that you unlawfully avoid from paying your income taxes or that you should be dishonest about your financial status when reporting it to the IRS. Although there are penalties for payment neglect, you should contact a tax specialist for advice and inquire about a course of action to take, before you allow your payments to lapse. There have been some cases that the IRS had permitted individuals with a payment agreement. They may allow you the same courtesy.

CHAPTER 5

Ways to Save Money While Unemployed

One suggestion that Mr. Smith and I would like to offer is that when you are grocery shopping, do not shop when you are hungry. We understand that many Americans usually do their grocery shopping while on their way home from work. If you have to shop while you are hungry, it would be beneficial to have a snack prior to entering the store. If you are hungry and see items that are appetizing to you at the moment, you will have a strong desire to purchase them. If you eye it, you'll buy it. Following are a few tips that have assisted us during our extreme cost-savings days.

At the Grocery Store: Your shopping strategy should not be designed around purchasing just the items that are on sale. Consideration should be given to saving time, money, and fuel. Your spending habits can have an affect on the funds that are dedicated to other household finances (mortgage, utility bills, and loans). Some of our suggestions would be to:
- Purchase store-brand items
- Use coupons when shopping
- Always shop for the lowest prices
- Purchase the necessary-sized items
- Purchase more prepared meals instead of fast foods
- Shop only at the supermarkets that will save you the most money
- When buying bulk quantities, shop at your nearest warehouse stores
- Make out your shopping list before you arrive at the supermarket, to avoid overspending

At Home: You can prevent spending hundreds of unnecessary dollars by seriously considering the follow cost-cutting tips:
- Avoid wasting food
- Improve your eating habits
- Change your furnace filter frequently
- Weather-strip your home to prevent air leaks
- Turn down your thermostat when using your fireplace
- Do not use excessive amounts of water and other utilities

- Reduce your cable channels to reduce your monthly cable bill
- Remember to turn off the lights in rooms that are not being used
- Shop for the best savings on your long-distance telephone service
- Close your curtains to eliminate heat from the sun, when using air conditioning
- Shop for bargains on all of your mortgage fees and homeowner rates with your lender
- Negotiate your activity membership fees, but if you cannot, cancel your membership

With Your Finances: During our financially impoverished days, Mr. Smith and I have learned over the years that it is okay if our family and friends are aware of our reduced income. However, one thing that we have never done is to broadcast our financial situation. When eating lunch with friends and having only enough cash for a salad, I would feel a little embarrassed. While looking at the menu, and before ordering my food, I would remark to my friends, "I only feel like having a salad, so let's do separate checks." This would inform my friends that I only want to pay for my meal. This truly works, so do not feel awkward about doing this. Following are helpful ways to save your money:
- Deposit your loose change in a jar on a daily basis
- Attend a garage or yard sale for immediate bargains
- Invest in the best insurance protection for your family
- Set aside an emergency fund for those unexpected expenses
- Have a garage or yard sale for unused items around your home
- Purchase generic drugs when buying over-the-counter medicine
- Continuing your education? Enroll in your local community college
- Never apply for a credit card that is not within your family's budget
- Before you proceed with legal assistance, ask for a free consultation first
- Shop around for the best interest rate at banks before opening an account
- Always pay your creditors within the time allotted to eliminate late charges
- Minimize your withdrawals from ATM machines to reduce transaction fees
- If you are at that golden age, never overlook senior citizen discount clubs and savings

- Request a semi-private room when admitted to a hospital to reduce medical expense
- Carry a higher deductible on your insurance policies to reduce your monthly payments
- Perform research at your local public library before spending money for legal assistance
- Find the best bargains through media ads before you spend your money on merchandise

While Traveling: Mr. Smith and I enjoy our planned vacations and our occasional spur-of-the-moment getaways, but before spending anything on a trip, we consider how much money we should allocate and how much money we need to return home with. While on a budget, we focus more on our spending and our schedule. The reason for spotlighting our schedule is to allot our time wisely so that we do not become too bored and look for places to visit, and eventually spend money unnecessarily. Reducing your travel and entertainment expenses is so valuable to your financial situation, and when you return home, you will be thankful that you followed your traveling plan. Some practical ideas to consider are:
- When traveling, avoid flying first-class
- Consider more fast-foods for their cost-saving prices
- When staying at a hotel, take advantage of the continental breakfast
- If your hotel room is equipped with a kitchen, try cooking for yourself
- Purchase your airline tickets in advance to avoid paying full-price fares
- Request a hotel room with a refrigerator, to store your purchased snacks and food
- While staying at a hotel for multiple nights, shop at a local grocery store for snacks
- Do not purchase the first souvenir items you find; check other vendors before buying them

With Your Vehicle: Fuel is becoming more and more expensive, and it is a scramble to find extra money to pay at the pump. Mr. Smith and I have compiled a few of our tips to help you save money on your vehicle expenses:
- Do not let your vehicle idle for long periods of time
- Utilize your cruise control unit to maintain the proper speed
- Fuel is very expensive, so try not to accelerate unnecessarily

- Do your own minor service and maintenance on your vehicle
- Inquire about a car-pool provider to reduce automobile expenses
- Inflate your auto tires to the proper weight to reduce gasoline usage
- Check your owner's manual for the proper fuel to use for your vehicle
- Unload excessive items from your vehicle. More weight uses more gas
- Invest in a vehicle that offers better mileage and lower maintenance costs
- Do not turn on your air conditioning, if the temperature does not warrant it
- Have a mechanic inspect any pre-owned vehicles before making a purchase
- Have your vehicle serviced for proper maintenance for fuel saving purposes
- Try negotiating the price of an automobile rather than paying the sticker price
- When making trips around town, complete multiple errands while you are out
- Make sure that your gas cap is secure because condensation can dilute your fuel
- Eliminate the high cost of a full-service station by filling up at a self-serve island
- Drive the posted speed limit, because the faster you drive, the more fuel you will use
- Change your motor oil every three thousand miles to lower the risk of engine damage

CHAPTER 6

Unemployment Insurance and Benefits

It would be wise to pursue the benefits that have been compiled for anyone who is unemployed or for anyone who is seeking better employment. Mrs. Smith and I discovered that by hiring a career counselor (whose services were free), we were introduced to a world of programs that we would not have otherwise encountered. Our counselor provided us with a self-assessment feedback form that gave us an idea of what we were eligible for and a few career interests that were very appropriate for us. There are several state and federally funded programs which provide funding and benefits for the single worker and for the head of a household, such as:

Child Daycare
Food Assistance
Health Care Benefits
Employment Services
Economic Stimulus Act
Social Welfare Programs
Veterans Assistance Programs
Section 8 Housing Assistance
Medicaid for Pregnant Women
WIC Programs (Women, Infants, Children)
Aid to Families with Dependent Children (AFDC)
Community Service Jobs for Older Americans
Vocational Training for the Disabled
Supplemental Aid to the Blind
Meals on Wheels for Seniors
Free School Lunch Programs
Unemployment Insurance
Job Placement Programs
Food Stamp Programs
Medicaid for Children
Educational Training
Energy Assistance
Nursing Care

For most individuals, their unemployment insurance is their only means of support, and although the compensation may not cover half of your bills, it keeps you from giving up.

CHAPTER 7

Tips for Applying for Unemployment

What exactly is unemployment insurance?
Unemployment insurance, or unemployment compensation, is a federal and state government-assistance program that provides temporary income for individuals who have become unemployed through no fault of their own; or for the employee who is looking for a new job. In most states, the compensation benefits last for approximately twenty-six weeks, and the benefit amount usually equals one-third of your base wages, provided that you have worked at least six months during the year prior to losing your job. With the new stimulus bill, many states have been allocated up to an additional thirteen weeks of unemployment benefits. Unemployment insurance is not deducted from the employee's paycheck, because employers pay the state for unemployment insurance benefits.

Who is eligible?
Qualified employees are covered under law by the unemployment insurance program, but there are exceptions. Every employee should ask their employer about unemployment insurance benefits and bylaws. Listed below are certain groups that may not participate in the unemployment insurance program:
- Elected officials
- Most nonprofit organizations
- Specific religious organizations
- Commissioned employers (real estate brokers or insurance agents)

Who can be disqualified for Unemployment?
Following are some of the conditions that may make you ineligible to collect unemployment benefits:
- Self-employed
- Resigned from your job without a good cause
- Resigned from your job because of bad health
- Terminated for deliberate disloyal performance

When can I begin to collect unemployment checks?
Each state has a waiting period before benefits can be received by the

claimant. After filing the initial claim, it usually takes three weeks before you receive your first check. The most reliable way to receive your weekly payment is by direct deposit to your bank account.

How do I apply for my benefits?

You may apply for unemployment compensation by contacting your state Division of Employment Security.

What information do I need when I apply?

Before calling or visiting your nearest unemployment office, you should gather the following information:

- Your birth date
- Your home address
- Your last day of employment
- Your Social Security Number
- Your home telephone number
- The explanation of your departure from your last employer
- Your alien registration information if you are not a U.S. citizen
- The names, birth dates, and Social Security Numbers for any dependent children
- Your work history contact information for all jobs within the past eighteen months
- Information on an unemployment insurance claim filed within the past eighteen months

How do I claim my weekly unemployment benefits?

You should promptly visit your nearest unemployment office or apply online. Applying online is the most efficient, because you can print out a receipt of your claim information and confirmation details.

What must I do to continue my eligibility?

To continue receiving benefits, you must be actively seeking full-time work, report any earnings that you have received during your claim weeks, and abide by each law and procedure established by the state.

Can I have a part-time job and receive benefits at the same time?

According to the laws in most states, yes you can. Your state determines the amount of unemployment compensation you may receive while working part-time. Before you begin working the ideal part-time job, you should investigate what unemployment benefits you can still receive during that time.

Can I collect severance pay and receive benefits at the same time?

In most states, you cannot collect severance pay and unemployment benefit payments during the same claim weeks.

Do my retirement payments, pension, or social security benefits have an effect on my unemployment benefits?
Yes, those payments may have an effect on the unemployment benefits you will receive.

If I quit my job, can I be eligible to collect unemployment benefits?
If you voluntarily quit your job, it is at the discretion of your former employer as to whether you are eligible. If for any reason you are disqualified, you have the right to file an appeal.

Will I be able to collect unemployment benefits if I am fired?
According to some state laws, you may be eligible. If you were terminated and your former employer is able to prove that you were fired for deliberate misbehavior, poor performance, or any company violations, you may not qualify.

Can I file for unemployment benefits if I was laid off twice within a year?
When your claim is filed, it remains on file for one year. Your claim can be reopened during this period, but is dependent on the unemployment benefit laws.

Am I required to pay taxes on my unemployment benefits?
Yes. Everyone is responsible for paying federal and state taxes on their unemployment benefits, and you can request to have them automatically withheld from your weekly benefit checks.

What if my spouse and I get laid off at the same time?
Both of you can file a claim, but only one of you can claim the dependency allowance.

What do I do if I receive an overpayment amount?
This does happen sometimes, and when it does, you will be required to repay the overpayment amount.

What do I do if I need to travel for an entire week during my unemployment claim period?

If you are out of town, unavailable to work, or not assertively searching for work, you cannot claim that week. If you happen to be out of town attending a job interview, you are eligible for benefits during the interview week.

What can I do when my unemployment benefits expire?

Remember, unemployment benefits are only temporary and should not be treated as steady income. It would be beneficial to file for benefits and begin seeking work during your first week of unemployment.

If I worked in multiple states, in which state should I file for unemployment benefits?

You must file your claim in each State.

How much weekly compensation am I eligible to receive?

Each state has different regulations to determine the weekly benefit amount for the qualified worker, and the benefit is based on that state's bylaws of financial assistance. Some states increase the benefit for families with children.

CHAPTER 8

Unemployment Benefit Payments

MAXIMUM WEEKLY BENEFITS PER STATE

Table 1	
Specific state information on Unemployment Insurance	
State	**Maximum**
Alabama	$255
Alaska	$370
Arizona	$240
Arkansas	$431
California	$450
Colorado	$487
Connecticut	$576
Delaware	$330
District of Columbia	$359
Florida	$275
Georgia	$330
Hawaii	$545
Idaho	$362
Illinois	$385
Indiana	$390
Iowa	$443
Kansas	$423
Kentucky	$415
Louisiana	$284
Maine	$496
Maryland	$380

Massachusetts	$628
Michigan	$365
Minnesota	$566
Mississippi	$230
Missouri	$320
Montana	$407
Nebraska	$308
Nevada	$362
New Hampshire	$427
New Jersey	$584
New Mexico	$455
New York	$405
North Carolina	$494
North Dakota	$385
Ohio	$372
Oklahoma	$392
Oregon	$482
Pennsylvania	$539
Rhode Island	$528
South Carolina	$326
South Dakota	$285
Tennessee	$275
Texas	$378
Utah	$444
Vermont	$409
Virginia	$378
Washington	$541
West Virginia	$424
Wisconsin	$363
Wyoming	$387

Note: All data displays the Unemployment Insurance maximum weekly claims.

Source. From *"Unemployment Insurance" (State Service Centers).* Copyright 2010 by The United States Department of Labor.

CHAPTER 9

Unemployment Divisions within the United States

Alabama
Alabama Department of Industrial Relations
866-234-5382
TTY: 800-499-2035
http://www.dir.alabama.gov

Alaska
Department of Labor and Workforce Development
888-252-2557
http://www.labor.state.ak.us

Arizona
Arizona Department of Economic Security
877-600-2722
TTY: 877-877-6226
https://www.azdes.gov/ASPNew/default.asp

Arkansas
Arkansas Department of Workforce Services
800-461-9941
TTY: 800-285-1131
http://www.arkansas.gov/esd/

California
California Employment Development Department
800-300-5616
TTY: 800-815-9387
http://www.edd.ca.gov/

Colorado
Colorado Department of Labor and Employment
800-388-5515
TTY: 303-318-9016 (within Denver) or TTY: 800-894-7730 (outside Denver)
http://www.coworkforce.com/uib/

Connecticut
Connecticut Department of Labor
800-942-6653
TTY: 800-842-9710
http://www.ctdol.state.ct.us/

Delaware
State of Delaware Department of Labor
800-794-3032
http://www.delawareworks.com/Unemployment/welcome.shtml

District of Columbia
DC Department of Employment Services
877-319-7346
http://www.does.dc.gov/does/site/default.asp

Florida
Florida Agency for Workforce Innovation
800-204-2418
http://www.floridajobs.org/

Georgia
Georgia Department of Labor
Within Atlanta 404-232-4290 or 404-232-3990
Outside Atlanta 866-873-5676
http://www.dol.state.ga.us/

Hawaii
Hawaii Department of Labor and Industrial Relations
877-215-5793
http://hawaii.gov/labor

Idaho
Idaho Department of Labor
208-332-3574
http://labor.idaho.gov/dnn/Default.aspx?alias=labor.idaho.gov/dnn/idl

Illinois
Illinois Department of Employment Security
888-367-4382
http://www.ides.state.il.us/

Indiana
Indiana Department of Workforce Development
888-967-5663
http://www.in.gov/dwd

Iowa
Iowa Workforce Development
866-239-0843
http://www.iowaworkforce.org/ui/

Kansas
Kansas Unemployment Insurance System
800-292-6333
TTY: 877-457-5432
https://www.uibenefits.dol.ks.gov/

Kentucky
Kentucky Office of Employment and Training
859-547-3362
http://www.des.ky.gov/

Louisiana
Louisiana Workforce Commission
866-783-5567
TTY: 800-259-5154
http://www.ldol.state.la.us/

Maine
Maine Department of Labor
800-593-7660
TTY: 888-457-8884
http://www.maine.gov/labor/

Maryland
Maryland Department of Labor, Licensing, and Regulation
410-368-5300
TTY: 410-767-2727 (within Baltimore) or TTY: 800-827-4400 (outside Baltimore)
http://www.dllr.state.md.us/

Massachusetts
Labor and Workforce Development
877-626-6800
TTY: 888-527-1912
http://www.mass.gov/?pageID=elwdhomepage&L=1&L0=Home&sid=Elwd

Michigan
Michigan Department of Labor & Economic Growth
866-500-0017
http://www.michigan.gov/uia

Minnesota
Minnesota Unemployment Insurance Program
877-898-9090
http://www.uimn.org/

Mississippi
Mississippi Department of Employment Security
888-844-3577
http://www.mdes.ms.gov/wps/portal

Missouri
Missouri Department of Labor and Industrial Relations
800-320-2519
TTY: 800-316-0896
http://www.dolir.mo.gov/

Montana
Montana Unemployment Insurance Division
406-247-1000
http://uid.dli.mt.gov/

Nebraska
Nebraska Workforce Development
877-725-9918
TTY: 402-471-0016
http://www.dol.state.ne.us/

Nevada
Nevada Department of Employment, Training and Rehabilitation
888-890-8211
TTY: 800-326-6868
http://detr.state.nv.us/

New Hampshire
New Hampshire Department of Employment Security
800-266-2252
TTY: 800-735-2964
http://www.nhes.state.nh.us/

New Jersey
New Jersey Department of Labor and Workforce Development
888-795-6672
TTY: 800-792-8339
http://lwd.state.nj.us/labor/index.shtml

New Mexico
New Mexico Department of Workforce Solutions
505-841-4000
http://www.dws.state.nm.us/

New York
New York State Department of Labor
888-209-8124 for New York State residents
877-358-5306 for out of state residents
TTY: 800-662-1220 and request the operator to call 888-783-1370
http://www.labor.state.ny.us/

North Carolina
Employment Security Commission of North Carolina
877-841-9617
https://www.ncesc.com/default.aspx

North Dakota
Job Service of North Dakota
701-328-4995
TTY 800-366-6888
http://jobsnd.com/

Ohio
Ohio Department of Job and Family Services
877-644-6562
http://jfs.ohio.gov/

Oklahoma
Oklahoma Employment Security Commission
800-555-1554
http://www.ok.gov/oesc_web/

Oregon
Oregon Employment Department
877-877-9996
http://www.emp.state.or.us/

Pennsylvania
Pennsylvania Department of Labor and Industry
888-313-7284
TTY: 888-334-4046
http://www.dli.state.pa.us/

Puerto Rico
787-625-7900
http://www.puertoricotrabaja.com

Rhode Island
Rhode Island Department of Labor and Training
866-557-0001
TTY: 401-243-9149
http://www.dlt.state.ri.us/

South Carolina
South Carolina Employment Security Commission
800-529-8339
http://www.sces.org/

South Dakota
South Dakota Department of Labor
605-626-3179
TTY: 800-877-1113
http://dol.sd.gov/

Tennessee
Tennessee Department of Labor and Workforce Development
877-813-0950
http://www.state.tn.us/labor-wfd/

Texas
Texas Workforce Commission
888-872-8417
TTY: 800-735-2989
http://www.twc.state.tx.us/

Utah
Utah Department of Workforce Services
888-848-0688
http://jobs.utah.gov/jobseeker/dwsdefault.asp

Vermont
Vermont Department of Labor
877-214-3330
TTY: 800-650-4152
http://www.vermont.gov/portal/employment/

Virginia
Virginia Employment Commission
866-832-2363
http://www.vec.virginia.gov/vecportal/

U.S. Virgin Islands
Department of Labor
St. Croix: 340-773-1440
All other Islands: 340-776-3700
http://www.vidol.gov/Units/Unemployment_Insurance/UI_TAXi.htm

Washington
Washington State Employment Security Department
800-318-6022
http://www.esd.wa.gov/

West Virginia
Workforce West Virginia
800-379-1032
TTY: 304-558-6840
https://www.workforcewv.org/

Wisconsin
Wisconsin Department of Workforce Development
800-822-5246
TTY: 888-393-8914
http://www.dwd.state.wi.us/ui/

Wyoming
Wyoming Department of Employment
866-729-7799
http://doe.state.wy.us/

CHAPTER 10

Unemployment Statistics

OCCUPATION EMPLOYMENT TOTALS

Table 2						
Totals for Employed and unemployed Americans						
(Numbers in thousands)	Employed		Unemployment		Unemployment %	
Occupation	Dec. 2008	Dec. 2009	Dec. 2008	Dec. 2009	Dec. 2008	Dec. 2009
Management, professional, and related occupations	52,548	52,131	1,802	2,509	3.3	4.6
Management, business, and financial operations	21,928	20,944	888	1,157	3.9	5.2
Professional and related occupations	30,619	31,188	915	1,352	2.9	4.2
Service occupations	24,371	24,216	2,057	2,747	7.8	10.2
Sales and office occupations	34,987	33,296	2,448	3,184	6.5	8.7
Sales and related occupations	16,354	15,478	1,233	1,520	7.0	8.9
Office and administrative support occupations	18,633	17,819	1,215	1,664	6.1	8.5
Natural resources, construction, and maintenance	14,202	12,617	2,063	2,802	12.7	18.2
Farming, fishing, and forestry occupations	901	869	201	242	18.3	21.8
Construction and extraction occupations	8,025	7,106	1,522	2,067	15.9	22.5

(Numbers in thousands)	Employed		Unemployment		Unemployment %	
Occupation	Dec. 2008	Dec. 2009	Dec. 2008	Dec. 2009	Dec. 2008	Dec. 2009
Installation, maintenance, and repair occupations	5,276	4,642	339	494	6.0	9.6
Production, transportation, and material moving	17,242	15,692	1,928	2,425	10.1	13.4
Transportation and material moving occupations	8,821	8,272	936	1,144	9.6	12.2

Source. From *"Employed and unemployed persons by occupation"* (Not seasonally adjusted). Copyright 2010 by The Bureau of Labor Statistics.

UNEMPLOYMENT RATES PER STATE

Table 3

Area Unemployment Statistics

Rank	State	Rate
1	NORTH DAKOTA	4.1%
2	NEBRASKA	4.5%
3	SOUTH DAKOTA	5.0%
4	KANSAS	6.3%
4	UTAH	6.3%
6	MONTANA	6.4%
6	VERMONT	6.4%
8	VIRGINIA	6.6%
9	IOWA	6.7%
9	LOUISIANA	6.7%
9	NEW HAMPSHIRE	6.7%
12	COLORADO	6.9%
13	HAWAII	7.0%

13	OKLAHOMA	7.0%
15	WYOMING	7.2%
16	ARKANSAS	7.4%
16	MARYLAND	7.4%
16	MINNESOTA	7.4%
19	NEW MEXICO	7.8%
20	MAINE	8.0%
20	TEXAS	8.0%
22	CONNECTICUT	8.2%
22	WISCONSIN	8.2%
24	WEST VIRGINIA	8.4%
25	DELAWARE	8.5%
25	PENNSYLVANIA	8.5%
27	NEW YORK	8.6%
28	ALASKA	8.7%
29	MASSACHUSETTS	8.8%
30	ARIZONA	8.9%
31	IDAHO	9.1%
32	WASHINGTON	9.2%
33	MISSOURI	9.5%
34	INDIANA	9.6%
34	MISSISSIPPI	9.6%
36	NEW JERSEY	9.7%
37	GEORGIA	10.2%
38	TENNESSEE	10.3%
39	ALABAMA	10.5%
40	KENTUCKY	10.6%
40	OHIO	10.6%
42	NORTH CAROLINA	10.8%
43	ILLINOIS	10.9%

44	OREGON	11.1%
45	FLORIDA	11.5%
46	DISTRICT OF COLUMBIA	11.8%
47	CALIFORNIA	12.3%
47	NEVADA	12.3%
47	SOUTH CAROLINA	12.3%
50	RHODE ISLAND	12.7%
51	MICHIGAN	14.7%

Notes: Rates shown are a percentage of the labor force. Data refer to place of residence. Estimates for the current month are subject to revision the following month.

Source. From *"Unemployment Rates for States" (Local Area Unemployment Statistics).* Copyright 2010 by The Bureau of Labor Statistics.

CHAPTER 11

Productive Things to Do While Unemployed

The following suggestions are listed as stress-free activities to discover, develop, and just enjoy, while deliberating your next career move. A fresh atmosphere can rejuvenate the reflections of your employment strategy and it can also create an awareness of the many entertaining occurrences that surround us. Mrs. Smith and I have taken advantage of many of the following activities:

ARTS & CRAFTS
Learn dancing:
Although we are usually just dancing spectators, Mrs. Smith believes that together we could enjoy ballroom dancing and maybe enter a contest or two. She also believes that this would be a great opportunity to meet new people and network for employment.

Learn sign language:
Learning sign language and tutoring someone who is deaf is a benefit to everyone involved—learning a new skill and time well spent helping another.

Learn a foreign language:
Mr. Smith has taken several trips outside the United States, and by learning the language of each country, he was able to communicate with the residents fluently.

Learn a new skilled trade:
During Mrs. Smith's most recent layoff, she attended challenging educational courses to acquire her pharmacy technician's license. She is now certified and has chosen this trade as her new career. I am proud that she devoted her unemployment time to commit to a successful profession.

Create your own greeting cards:
Mrs. Smith and I have been designing our own personal greeting cards for years. Not only does this save us money, but it allows us to put our own personal touch into each card.

AUTOMOBILE
Take a weekend getaway:
On several occasions, Mr. Smith and I would take the kids and travel one-hundred to two-hundred miles from home and enjoy a short vacation. This was his way of escaping and refreshing his thoughts regarding employment. This truly helped him.

Understand gas-saving tips:
Within the past couple of years, gasoline prices have fluctuated so much that it is impossible to know how much fuel will cost on a daily basis. It would be wise to comprehend how the costs will affect your budget.

Learn to do minor repairs and services on your car:
Many times, Mr. Smith would change the oil, replace the spark plugs and perform other minor services on our vehicles, which would save money and keep him occupied.

BEAUTY
Create a different hairstyle:
Sometimes a new hairdo can be a new you. Changing your style can help change your outlook on your employment approach.

Learn to groom and style your own hair to save at salons:
While laid off, Mrs. Smith has saved the family money by learning to style and groom our children's hair.

COMPUTERS
Practice typing:
Mrs. Smith practiced typing so often that she became proficient enough to teach others.

Learn how they work:
Possessing computer knowledge is a great tool for potential employment.

Use the Internet to correspond with someone:
Searching for a job online is better than standing in an employment line.

COUNSELING
Assist a needy person:
When you give generously, you are applying assistance to someone who desires it. We often think about the times when others assisted us in our times of need, and we contribute to those who require the essentials.

Volunteer and assist at a suicide-prevention center or an abuse center:
Mr. Smith has provided support at our local suicide-prevention center. One of the young men that he volunteered to help is now a good family friend. The young man now has a great focus on life.

EDUCATION
Tutor someone:
You can encourage someone by sharing your knowledge and experience and assisting them with a subject that they are having trouble with. It will help you and the individual, now and later in life.

Complete or further your education:
Education is the key to promotional employment and self accomplishment. Mr. Smith is currently taking several online courses to increase his knowledge.

ENTERTAINMENT
Enter a contest:
There are many free contests offered by organizations that present prizes and money to the winners.

Practice dramatic acting:
Learning or enhancing public speaking techniques can inspire an individual to feel confident when communicating in a public domain.

Cut down on entertainment expense:
Cutting back on entertainment is important, especially to anyone who has a fixed income or is having problems paying bills on time.

Attend the afternoon matinee instead of shows playing at night:
Many movie theaters offer shows all day and night and you would pay extra for tickets for the evening shows. We usually attend a movie before 5:00 PM to save $2 to $3 on each ticket.

Go on a picnic instead of to a restaurant:
While unemployed, Mr. Smith and I regularly enjoyed outings to some of the many public parks in our area. This increased our time together and saved on restaurant expenses.

Turn off the television:
Designate three to five hours one day a week with no television Use this time to improve and develop your personal and professional skills.

FAMILY LIFE
Bond with your children:
Spending time with your children, either in person or over the telephone is time very well spent. Children can be a great comfort.

Renew your wedding vows:
Revitalizing your relationship with your spouse creates reassurance and togetherness. An incredible mate can be a great comfort when out of work.

Complete your last will and testament:
The idea of implementing this legal declaration is unsettling, but it is effective in identifying your personal property status for you and your loved ones.

Get better acquainted with family and friend:
There is a great comfort in being close to family and friends. Mrs. Smith and I keep in frequent contact with our family and friends, and we strongly suggest staying in touch with loved ones, especially following a job loss.

FOOD
Eat correctly:
For many unemployed individuals, diet is last on the list of things to consider. While unemployed, some lose weight, and some gain weight. We suggest budgeting your food costs to include good nutritional cuisine and proper eating habits. A healthy heart and healthy mind can keep you focused on your future.

Create a recipe:
This can be a lot of creative fun, and it could bring new imagination to your thought-development process. While unemployed, Mrs. Smith truly inspired both of us by creating a new meal idea and preparing it herself.

Bake a cake (men):
Although Mr. Smith cooks dinner for the family frequently, he rarely bakes cakes; but when he does, it *usually* turns out pretty good. He would prepare meals for the family when I was the only breadwinner, and this allowed him to stay active and creative.

HEALTH
Donate blood:
Your blood donation can make a difference between life and death.

Donations help save lives, and many individuals donate primarily because it makes them feel good to know that they can make a difference.

Get a physical:
Make an appointment with a doctor and get a physical. A potential employer is more likely to hire an emotionally and physically healthy individual.

Exercise correctly:
A proper exercise routine will eventually produce results, and boost your self-esteem. Stay in shape while seeking employment.

Quit all bad habits:
Everyone has some type of habit or addiction that they wish would go away. There are lesser habits: consuming junk food, nail biting, or overeating; and then there are the more serious habits: alcohol, drugs, or tobacco. Any of the more serious habits may prevent you from acquiring your next job. It would be healthier for you and your career to end all bad habits.

Improve personal hygiene:
Careful and continuous grooming is very important for anyone who is seeking employment. Good hygiene and personal appearance are keys to your success.

Understand your bodily functions:
Every person should be aware of common disorders and operations of their body. Example: During the stress of unemployment, a person may develop uncomfortable physical symptoms. It would be beneficial to know what to do when the discomfort occurs.

Select a personal or family physician:
Unemployed individuals may not have health benefits. If possible, prior to the expiration of any current benefits, locate and familiarize yourself with a physician. When you do find employment, then you will already have an established relationship with a physician.

HOME
Recycle:
We should always continue to improve our recycling practices by salvaging our paper products. Recycling also helps control our waste disposal problems.

Plant a tree:
You can be ecologically friendly and increase natural beauty. The newly

planted tree can represent your new outlook on your employment future, and it can be a perfect way to honor the new you.

House cleaning:
As the saying goes, "an uncluttered home is an uncluttered mind". This is definitely true. With a clean home, you can lay your résumés and employment documents anywhere, and you will be able to easily locate them. If your home is untidy and cluttered, you may never find those résumés and documents until after the position has been filled by another applicant.

Have a yard sale:
Extra cash is always good. A yard sale can also help clear your home of those unnecessary items. Mr. Smith and I never realized how many items that we had collected over the years (kid's toys, VCR's, books, etc.) until we decided to assemble them all together for our yard sale. We were overwhelmed with the number of collectibles, and with the money received from the sale.

Redecorate or rearrange your home:
Give your home a makeover. A different environment can reflect your new future.

Create a library with collected books:
Organize your books. Reading books can keep your mind occupied, but only if you know where to find them.

Organize all documents & warranties:
Manage and organize all of your household records, owner's manuals, warranties, and receipts. You will be able to quickly locate these important documents when you need them. This can also improve your organizational skills.

Clean exterior of home (awnings and gutters):
When you improve the appearance of your home on the outside, you'll be filled with satisfaction on the inside.

JOB-RELATED
Update your résumé:
Your résumé should state who you are, where you have been, and where you are going.

Practice interviewing skills:
Practice before going for live interviews. Mr. Smith would organize a simulated interview session for me during my employment searches, and he would ask difficult questions and scenarios that would keep me alert during the process. Some of the questions that he had asked me during our sessions were questions that some of the interviewers asked me during my live interviews. This honestly prepared me, and I gained self-confidence.

Inquire and apply for government aid:
Government benefits are there to assist citizens across America. There are valuable government opportunities like Social Security and Medicare, but you may be eligible for several of other federal and state-assisted programs.

Apply for unemployment compensation:
As soon as a worker is laid off, that individual should apply for unemployment. Your employer should supply you with a separation package, usually on your last day of work. There should be information and instructions on how to file your unemployment claim. Our compensation was a blessing, especially after our severance pay was exhausted.

Explore other professions:
You already know who you are; now it is time to discover who you can be. Mr. Smith and I have changed our professions and are happy with our choices.

MILITARY
Inquire about enlisting opportunities:
Although this may not pertain to every laid-off employee, there are still those that fall within the enlistment age range of seventeen to forty-two years old. We may not see how the job market will generate employment for the future, and military service may be an option. Remember, the military is not a job program, but instead, it is an opportunity to serve our country.

MONEY
Save and use coupons:
Mrs. Smith is known in our family as the "Coupon Queen". She has saved us money on grocery bills, restaurant meals, merchandise and many other items by using coupons. Every Saturday night, Mrs. Smith purchases the early edition of the Sunday paper and goes through the sales and coupon

pages. She has taught our family that the best thing to do when spending your own money is to present a piece of paper that says "½ off" or "free".

Explore the financial program that is right for you:
It would be beneficial for you and your family to understand which investments are yielding the best return. Retirement plans, 401k programs and savings tactics are some of the effective ways to improve your finances. To understand financial investing is an educational and personal experience that every person should be familiar with, especially with regard to their own finances. There are many effective tools and techniques that can educate you to become more successful with your assets.

Give to a benevolent fund:
There are many benevolent funds available, so choosing just one of them may be a difficult decision. Whichever amount you desire to donate, $3, $4, or even $5 per month, the donation covers a qualifying victim of natural disasters, national emergencies, individuals that require medical assistance, and families in need of basic food, clothing and housing. As a member, you are also qualified to receive donations and assistance.

Balance your checkbook:
This should be a monthly process. Mr. Smith and I prefer to do our banking online, and we verify our expenses each week. This helps us to know where our money is going and how much of it remains.

Budget your money wisely:
This was a very difficult task for both of us, more than ever when one of us was laid off. During Mr. Smith's first layoff, budgeting was not our specialty; and with two small children, we decided to request some professional assistance. We turned to Consumer Credit Counseling to help us with our mortgage, late credit card fees, auto loans, and other finances. They were able to provide us with a financial plan and supportive resources. The best part about Consumer Credit Counseling is that there was no fee for their services.

Organize your accounts and bills:
Receiving a "past due" bill in your mailbox is disheartening, especially when you forgot to pay the bill. Mr. Smith and I have preset reminders on our cell phones for when a bill is due. Our reminders alert us a couple of days before the actual due date.

Learn to file your own income taxes:
This can save you money that you would generally pay to the tax preparer.

Learning this trade could be a skill that you could perform for others, and you would be paid at the same time.

Inquire about cleaning up your credit:
One of the most important tasks that you can do for your future is to take care of your credit. Your credit scores will follow you for years. Stay in constant contact with your creditors, and keep them informed of your financial status. Most creditors understand situations of the unemployed, and they may consider giving you assistance.

Read and learn from the *Wall Street Journal*:
Recognizing international business, financial news, and their issues is identifying with our economy. Learning our market behavior is the groundwork for understanding where our money is going.

Freeze credit cards for three months:
This is a technique that has worked for us. Not only can you freeze your credit cards, but you can also freeze your credit file. Freezing your credit file means that your credit becomes unavailable to potential lenders, employers, and credit card issuers. This is very helpful for those that use their credit cards in unnecessary ways.

MUSIC
Join a choir:
This is an opportunity to create new friendships and make a joyful noise. Singing with others is a beautiful thing, and it can help restore your soul.

Write a song:
Everyone has a song to sing, and pouring your heart and soul into your personal song could be incredible therapy.

Learn to play a musical instrument:
Beginning instrumental music participation can speed up your learning. You can spend idle time studying for this new activity, and you just may find that it is worth it. After Mr. Smith returned from an employment search, he would unwind by playing soft music on his guitar—sometimes for hours. This helped him to relax and take a break from the frustrations of employment pursuits.

OTHER ACTIVITIES
Attend a wedding you've been invited to:
Weddings are beautiful and joyous. Everyone looks so happy and beautiful, and you can join in on the fun.

Attend your reunion:
Although reunions are infrequent, if you have the time to attend an upcoming event, you can use this opportunity as an outing to network for potential future employment.

Expand your vocabulary:
A person is more professional when he can express his thoughts and ideas in an enhanced manner.

Visit your neighbors:
Paying a quick visit to your neighbors can provide emotional simulation to you and your neighbor. Volunteering to assist them can also be rewarding. Mr. Smith and I have elderly neighbors that we communicate with monthly, and when a special occasion arises (holidays, birthdays, parties, etc.), we usually visit them to show support.

Carry out your promises:
Prepare a list of positive and constructive pledges to accomplish. These activities should have the makings of encouraging achievements.

PUBLIC
Vote:
Mr. Smith and I feel that it is very important to take part in elections, either as a candidate or just casting a ballot for a public official. For those that are registered voters, this is a valuable and powerful opportunity to display your concerns and interest in your community.

Adopt a highway:
Not only can you become a conscious citizen contributing to a cleaner environment, but you, or your affiliated organization, can be recognized for your commitment. This is a great way to assist a community.

Visit your library:
There are mountains of books that can refresh and rejuvenate a person's spirit. Although you can find just about any topic to read about on the Internet, there is a great sentiment in holding a paperback or hardcover book.

Understand your United States Constitution:
It is important for all Americans to comprehend the U.S. Constitution. It contains our citizen rights, supreme laws, and the structure of our country. Many Americans may not know that employment policies are mentioned in the Constitution, such as the "At-Will Employment" doctrine. Mr. Smith

and I both currently work for employers that practice this doctrine, and we thoroughly understand the principles and guidelines of their practices.

Help beautify your community:
Over the years, our communities may show some deterioration, but it takes someone who has a little time and ambition to help restore the beauty.

Support your local police department:
Our police officers are the primary guardians of our society and neighborhoods, and when we "Back the Badge", we contribute our time and goodwill to the force.

RELIGION
Pay your tithes or offerings:
Many people feel that giving their tithes or offerings to the church (while on a tight budget or laid off) is an impractical suggestion. Although giving to the church is voluntary, it is intended to be a joy and a blessing. You will be planting a seed for your future when you give from the heart.

Attend church or mass:
When you worship and give thanks to God, you are placing your trust in him for guidance. He has never failed anyone, and he will not fail you.

Become active in a church:
There are many ways to serve in a religious setting: you can teach, preach, sing, or just be of assistance to someone who requires aid.

SELF HELP
Read a novel:
Sometimes, quiet moments can thrill the soul after a busy day, and a good novel can help you unwind.

Obtain a healthy hobby:
Since we started exercising, power walking, and jogging together, we have been able to help keep a balance between our employment searches and our agitation of not finding work. Exercising together is like a long pleasant journey with a friend. This was very therapeutic with helping to calm our unemployment anxiety.

Write your bibliography:
Everyone has a story to tell, and it is disappointing that many never tell it. By writing about your life, you can rediscover who you are and the valuable

life lessons that you have learned along the way. The key is to inform yourself and others of the quality and strength of your resources.

Define and position your priorities:
Knowing your priorities will help you focus on where you are headed. Your priorities should be your personal fulfillment arrangement and the precedence it represents in your life. The priority list below is what Mrs. Smith and I follow daily:

1. God
2. Spouse
3. Children
4. Family and Friends
5. Home
6. Career

Set and achieve your personal goals:
Without personal goals, a person cannot follow a path to success. Achievable goals and a balanced plan should be established.

VOLUNTEER
Be an assistant at a food shelter:
When you volunteer to help feed the hungry, you are providing assistance to someone who may have also lost their job. Encouraging others displays respect and compassion. For many years, Mr. Smith was a volunteer delivery driver at a food pantry, and he would distribute perishable foods to the local resource centers.

Be an assistant at a housing shelter:
There are many different jobs and tasks within housing shelters where you can lend your talents: building repair, caretaker, custodian, electrician, curator, or plumber. You can play an important role in helping others to develop themselves.

Be a supporter of the Big Brothers and Big Sisters of America:
We have a very good friend who has supported this organization for many years, and he and his wife have developed lasting relationships with the children in the mentoring program. They have made a difference and an impact on the lives of these children.

Remember, each of us has twenty-four hours to accomplish something everyday, but it is up to us to spend our time wisely.

CHAPTER 12

The Importance of an Educated Employee

Mrs. Smith and I believe that the importance of education is quite clear. It is the means of absorbing the full potential of knowledge and to incorporate the teachings that will help generate concepts, which will inspire others. Education is the property for which relevant information allows us to be useful, practical and creative. Whether you have a High School education or you are a college graduate, the experiences and correspondence that you have collected are designed to help prepare you for the working environment. We embrace both of our children and emphasize to them of the importance of higher education in order for them to prime themselves for the many challenges and opportunities of adulthood and employment. By inspiring children early in life of the significance of learning in school, each will carry with them this effective impression through employment and through life. On my job, many of my coworkers who are well educated are also leaders, managers and principle decision makers within the company. This does not mean that a person has to have a good education to be a leader, manager or a director, but it can help achieve their employment goal, as it has with my coworkers. There is tremendous value with receiving a good education, because not only can a person successfully meet their goals and expectations, but an employer will take notice and may appoint you a leading position to help meet the company's goals and expectations. The more celebrated detail (education) provided in your life, the better participation opportunities (employment) may be provided to you. A good education is an experience not to be missed.

If you have the desire to expand your learning ability by earning a college degree and if you have the means for college, then I would suggest that you truly consider enrolling at a local community college or at a university. For those who feel that they do not have enough hours in the day to go to class or they feel that going to college is too expensive, I have to say that "**it can be done**". We understand that there are many working parents who feel that their home life, full-time work and personal life demands too many hours throughout the day, but consider the impact that your future will benefit from your education. Our book *Mr. and Mrs. Smith's Employment Survival Guide* was completed in 6 months of extreme research and planned writing, and during this time: I was a full-time student attending online courses at the University of Phoenix, working 50 hours per week with my employer, performing my fatherly duties, being a full-time husband, taking care of my household responsibilities and focusing on writing full time. This was the most laborious tasks in unison that I have ever performed. What kept me going? I placed every aspect of my tasks in order of importance.

1. God
2. Spouse
3. Children
4. Family
5. Home
6. Career
7. Education
8. Survival Guide

By following this order, I was able to concentrate and direct my energy to this book. Yes, I did attend school during the production of the book; because I wanted to take some classes to help sharpen my writing skills. After researching our local colleges and the writing courses that they offered, I visited the University of Phoenix and enrolled in their Effective Writing and Research Writing courses. I was so impressed with the instructors and methods of learning that I also enrolled in the following courses: Contemporary Communications, Human Resources Management and Marketing. Each of these courses has prepared me with the education, knowledge and comprehension to introduce this book to you. Mrs. Smith and I want to provide to each of our readers of the magnitude of informational knowledge that we have attained through training and education. "**It can be done**".

I have heard many people state that "college is not for me" or "why is it so important to continue my education?" My response to these remarks is "a higher education can immediately generate a higher income". Then there is the statement "I can't afford to go to college and my daytime workload demands too much time". If time is an issue during your day, then you may consider evening classes or online courses that many colleges and universities offer, of which you can set your own schedule to. There are online colleges that offer an Associates degree for under $20,000, and if you are eligible, you can receive financial aid from one of several government educational grants. It would be wise to seek the assistance of a financial counselor, preferably from the college or university that you are considering attending. Before taking these courses, I had been out of school for over 20 years and my recent return to the university level brought back some memorable thoughts of my days as a Central Missouri State University freshman, watching the students studying while lying on the grass in the quadrangle, and seeing other students doing homework in the student center. **"It can be done"**.

When I decided to return to school, I knew that I would feel like the old man in class, but when I discovered the online courses and how I could study at an undemanding pace, I immediately enrolled. I received great student financial advice from my enrollment counselor as she introduced me to the Free Application for Federal Student Aid (FAFSA). This program analyzed my personal information and calculated my eligibility for all forms of government financial aid. Although I could have selected from many other accredited schools, I selected the University of Phoenix because of its proximity and the great feedback that I received from others who had attended.

There are other outstanding online schools that I had researched and considered attending, such as:

Abilene Christian University
http://www.acu.edu

American Sentinel University
http://www.americansentinel.edu

Ashford University
http://www.ashford.edu

Ashworth College
http://www.ashworthcollege.edu

AT Still University
http://www.atsu.edu

Boston University
http://www.bu.edu

Bowling Green State University
http://www.bgsu.edu

Bryant and Stratton College
http://www.bryantstratton.edu

California Coast University
http://www.calcoast.edu

California University of Pennsylvania
http://www.cup.edu

Capella University
http://www.capella.edu

City University
http://www.cityu.edu

Colorado Technical University
http://www.coloradotech.edu

Concord Law School
http://www.concordlawschool.edu

ECPI College of Technology
http://www.ecpi.edu

Everest College Phoenix
http://www.everest.edu

Everest University
http://www.everest.edu

Florida Tech University
http://www.floridatechonline.com

Grand Canyon University
http://online.gcu.edu

International Career School/Canada
http://www.icslearn.com

Iowa Central College
http://www.iowacentral.edu

ITT Technical Institute
http://itt-tech.edu

Jones International University
http://jonesinternational.edu/

Kaplan University
http://www.Kaplan.edu

LA College
http://www.lac.edu

Liberty University
http://www.liberty.edu

Lincoln College of Technology
http://www.lincolnedu.com

National American University
http://www.national.edu

New England College
http://www.nec.edu

Northeastern University
http://www.northeastern.edu

Norwich University
http://www.norwich.edu

Penn Foster College
http://www.pennfostercollege.edu

Pinnacle Career Institute
http://www.pcitraining.edu

Saint Leo University
http://www.saintleo.edu

San Joaquin Valley College
http://www.sjvc.edu

Stetson University
http://www.stetson.edu

The George Washington University
http://www.gwu.edu

Tiffin University
http://www.tiffin.edu

University of Maryland University College
http://www.umuc.edu

University of Phoenix
www.phoenix.edu

University of the Rockies
http://www.rockies.edu

Upper Iowa University
http://www.uiu.edu

Utica College
http://www.utica.edu

Virginia College
www.vc.edu

Walden University
http://www.waldenu.edu

Western Governors University
http://www.wgu.edu

Western International University
http://www.west.edu

Westwood College
http://www.westwood.edu

CHAPTER 13

Financial Assistance

After narrowing your choices of schools and comparing the different academic courses offered and their cost, it is now time to carefully select financial assistance. You may want to speak with a financial counselor at each of the schools that you have selected, as they will provide you with the necessary documentation and direction that is suitable for your financial status. Below is a list of financial organizations that can also provide guidance to education financing assistance.

Academics and Athletes (Natl Collegiate Athletic Association)
http://www2.ncaa.org/portal/academics_and_athletes
NCAA's Student-Athlete page is filled with useful info to help students stay eligible to compete, make the right choices about their health, perform in the classroom, and develop into tomorrow's leaders.

American Foreign Service Association's HS Essay Contest
http://www.afsa.org/essaycontest/
Open to all HS students whose parents are not in the US Foreign Service.

American Indian College Fund (AICF)
http://www.collegefund.org
Student scholarships and other developmental needs at the nation's tribal colleges and universities across the United States.

American Indian Science and Engineering Society (AISES)
http://www.aises.org
A national, nonprofit organization which bridges science and technology with traditional Native American values, encouraging studies in science, engineering, and other academic areas with scholarships, internships & other programs.

California Governor's Scholarship Programs (State of California)
http://www.cagovernorsscholars.org
California students who demonstrate high academic achievement in math and sciences can earn scholarships for college from the state.

College.gov
http://www.college.gov/wps/portal
The source for information and resources about planning, preparing and paying for education beyond high school.

College Access
http://going2college.org/StateResources/
Provides all the resources your state has on preparing for college, planning a career, finding and applying to college and what state aid is available to help pay for college.

Educational Partnership Program (NOAA)
http://epp.noaa.gov
Financial help for minority promising scientists.

Educational Service Centers (League of United Latin American Citizens)
http://www.lnesc.org
Provides the Hispanic community with high-quality educational opportunities.

FAFSA (US Dept of Education)
http://www.fafsa.ed.gov
Assists with applying for federal financial aid online.

FastWeb.com Scholarship Search
http://www.fastweb.com/index.ptml
Provides access to a free online database to locate and apply for college scholarships.

Federal Employee Education and Assistance Fund
http://www.feea.org
A private, non-profit corporation which provides educational benefits and emergency assistance to all civilian and postal federal employees and their dependent family members.

Financial Aid Resources - Dept of Defense Education Activity
http://www.dodea.edu/instruction/curriculum/Financial%20Aid/
FinancialAid.htm
The Financial Aid Resources page from the Department of Defense
Education Activity (DODEA) provides information available to military
dependents.

Funding Education Beyond High School (US Dept of Education)
http://studentaid.ed.gov/students/publications/student_guide/index.html
Information center for college planning.

High School Journalism (American Society of Newspaper Editors)
http://www.highschooljournalism.org
This site is to encourage a diverse generation of young people to make
newspaper journalism their career.

Hispanic Serving Institutions National Program (US Dept of Agriculture)
http://www.hsi.usda.gov
Provides professional development opportunities to students, faculty and
staff at HSI's with internships, scholarships, grants, fellowships and more.

Imagine America Scholarship (Career College Association)
http://www.imagine-america.org
A program that can help fund your education, and also help you make the
big decisions - like choosing a career.

International Education Financial Aid (IEFA)
http://www.iefa.org
Offers a free searchable database of scholarships specifically for international
students wishing to study in a foreign country.

Jeannette Rankin Women's Education Fund
http://www.rankinfoundation.org
Awards scholarships annually to women 35 years of age and older who
through undergraduate or vocational education.

KnowHow2GO
http://www.knowhow2go.org/
Provides middle school students to adults the extensive information on the
value of continuing education after high school, how to prepare for college,
the myths vs. realities about college and the availability of financial aid
for college.

NASA For Students (Natl Aeronautics & Space Administration)
http://www.nasa.gov/audience/forstudents/postsecondary/features/index.html
A Students Page filled with multimedia, interactive features, and fascinating facts, plus NASA competitions, internships, careers, scholarships, current research, and much more.

Nursing Information (US Bureau of Health Professions)
http://bhpr.hrsa.gov/nursing
Resource for anyone considering a career in nursing.

Opportunity.gov
http://federalstudentaid.ed.gov/opportunity/index.html
New Educational Opportunities for Unemployed Workers.

Paying For College (Collegeboard.com)
http://www.collegeboard.com/student/pay/index.html
Assists with locating financial aid with advice from the College Board's experts and interactive tools.

Scholarship Scams (US Federal Trade Commission)
http://www.ftc.gov/bcp/conline/edcams/scholarship/index.html
This site cautions students on how to discover fraud.

Scholarship Search (Collegeboard.com)
http://apps.collegeboard.com/cbsearch_ss/welcome.jsp
Locate scholarships, loans, internships, and other financial aid programs from non-college sources that match your education level, talents, and background.

Scholarships & Internships (US Dept of Energy)
http://www.energy.gov/scholarships%26internships.htm
Information on scholarships, internships and competitions from the U.S. Dept of Energy.

Scholarships and Loan Repayment Program (Indian Health Services)
http://www.ihs.gov/JobsCareerDevelop/DHPS/Scholarships/index.html
Indian Health Service's scholarships for American Indian health professionals.

Scholarships - Society of Women Engineers (SWE)
http://societyofwomenengineers.swe.org/index.php
Supports to stimulate women to achieve their full potential in careers as engineers and leaders.

Student Aid on the Web (US Dept of Education)

http://www.studentaid.ed.gov

Tools to assist a student who is applying for federal financial aid.

Student Assistance Programs (US Dept of Health and Human Services)

http://bhpr.hrsa.gov/dsa/index.htm

Provides scholarships, loans and loan repayment programs for students in the health professions.

Student Services, National Association of Black Journalists (NABJ)

http://www.nabj.org/programs/scholarships/index.php

Seeks to strengthen ties among African-American journalists, promote diversity in newsrooms, and honor excellence in journalism.

Student Volunteering (US Dept of Veterans Affairs)

http://www.volunteer.va.gov/StudentProgram.asp

This program allows students to explore health care career options and offer scholarship opportunities to student volunteers.

Total and Permanent Disability (TPD) Discharge - DOED

http://disabilitydischarge.ed.gov

A resource center for Total and Permanent Disability (TPD) discharge of the federal student loans and the service obligation of Teacher Education Assistance for Higher Education (TEACH) Grants.

United Negro College Fund (UNCF)

http://www.uncf.org

A national advocate for the importance minority higher education by representing the public policy interests of its students.

CHAPTER 14

Scholarship Foundations

Another way of receiving financial assistance for a higher education is through scholarship foundations, of which awards are given by private programs, federal affiliations and associate partners of exclusive organizations. These scholarships are usually of a moderate monetary value, but they offer some relief from the tuition balance. Scholarships are presented to motivate the recipient to promote their field of study, but there are factors taken into consideration which determine the awards to each recipient who qualify, such as: national origin, race, religion or maintaining a certain GPA. Below are a few notable scholarship organizations.

Agricultural Science Scholarships (Future Farmers of America)
http://www.ffa.org/index.cfm?method=c_programs.Scholarships
Scholarships to members with career goals in agricultural programs.

American Library Association Scholarship Program
http://www.ala.org/ala/educationcareers/education/scholarships/index.cfm
Awarded to students who are pursuing a Masters in Library Science (MLS).

American Society for Enology and Viticulture Scholarships
http://asev.org/scholarship-program
The American Society awards scholarships to students pursuing a degree in enology, viticulture, or in a curriculum emphasizing a science basic to the wine and grape industry.

Anne Ford Scholarship
http://www.ncld.org/content/view/725/508
The Anne Ford Scholarship is a ten thousand dollar award given to a high school senior with an identified learning disability (LD) who is pursuing an undergraduate degree.

Automation Alley Scholarships (Michigan)

http://www.automationalley.com/autoalley/Get+Involved/
Education+and+Training/Scholarships.htm

This program offers scholarships to employees or family members of Michigan's "Automation Alley" member companies.

Aviation Education Scholarships & Grants (US Federal Aviation Administration)

http://www.faa.gov/education_research/education/student_resources/
scholarships_grants/index.cfm

Government and private scholarships for aviation students.

Barry M. Goldwater Scholarship and Excellence in Education Program

http://www.act.org/goldwater

For outstanding students who pursue careers in math, science or engineering.

Benjamin A. Gilman International Scholarship Program (US Dept of State)

http://www.iie.org//programs/gilman/index.html

This scholarship provides awards for U.S. undergraduate students who are receiving federal Pell Grant funding at a 2-year or 4-year college or university to participate in study abroad programs worldwide.

Coca-Cola Scholarships

https://www.coca-colascholars.org/cokeWeb/jsp/scholars/Index.jsp

For those special students who exemplify the potential to become the leaders of tomorrow.

DUSA Scholarships

http://www.dodea.edu/students/dusa.htm

The Society of Daughters of the U.S. Army (DUSA) offers $1,000 scholarships to the daughters and granddaughters of active duty or retired Army officers.

Ernest F. Hollings Undergraduate Scholarship Program

http://www.oesd.noaa.gov/Hollings_info.html

The National Oceanic and Atmospheric Administration (NOAA) Ernest F. Hollings scholarship provides undergraduate awards to interns at a NOAA facility.

Federal Cyber Service: Scholarship for Service (Natl Science Foundation)
http://www.nsf.gov/funding/pgm_summ.jsp?pims_id=5228%26org=NSF
Undergraduate or graduate education in exchange for two years of federal service after graduation.

Gates Millennium Scholarship Program (GMS)
http://www.gmsp.org
Provides African Americans, Native Americans, Asian Pacific Americans, and Hispanic Americans with scholarships for study in mathematics, science, engineering, education or library science.

Hispanic Scholarship Fund
http://www.hsf.net
The largest Hispanic scholarship-granting organization in the nation.

Indian Health Service Scholarships & Loan Repayment Programs
http://www.ihs.gov/JobsCareerDevelop/DHPS/LRP/lrpsc.asp
Awards to students in exchange for two years of full-time clinical practice at an approved Indian health program.

Jack Kent Cooke Foundation Scholarship
http://www.jackkentcookefoundation.org
Scholarships to undergraduate students who have completed at least a year of school.

Minority Engineering Scholarships (NACME)
http://www.nacme.org/scholarships
Scholarships for African American, American Indian, & Latino women and men in engineering.

National Eagle Scout Scholarships
http://www.nesa.org/
The Boy Scouts of America scholarships for Eagle Scouts.

National Merit Scholarships
http://www.nationalmerit.org
Undergraduate National Merit scholarships.

Nevada Millennium Scholarship (Nevada State Treasurer)
https://nevadatreasurer.gov/index.html
Graduates of Nevada high schools who have been state residents for at least two of their high school years may be eligible for the Governor Guinn Millennium Scholarship.

Presidential Freedom Scholarship
http://www.learnandserve.gov/about/programs/pfs.asp
Awards $1,000 scholarships to high school juniors or seniors selected by their schools for outstanding service to their community.

Robert C. Byrd Honors Scholarship Program
http://www.ed.gov/programs/iduesbyrd/index.html
Is designed to recognize exceptionally able high school seniors who show promise of continued excellence in postsecondary education.

Scholarship Search (US Dept of Education)
http://studentaid2.ed.gov/getmoney/pay_for_college/types_scholarships.html
A program which ensures all eligible individuals benefit from federal financial assistance.

Scholarships (NGPA)
http://www.ngpa.org/content.aspx?page_id=22&club_id=189069&module_id=21635
An education fund established to provide educational assistance in the form of scholarships to members of the gay and lesbian community who are interested in an aviation career as a professional pilot.

Scholarships - Association of Former Special Agents of the IRS
http://www.afsa-irs.org/Scholar.htm
Scholarships to students pursuing a degree in law enforcement or related fields such as business or accounting.

Scholarships for Military Children
http://www.militaryscholar.org
Scholarships for military sons and daughters of U.S. military personnel.

Scholarships, Organization of Chinese Americans (OCA)
http://www.ocanational.org/index.php?option=com_content&task=view&id=59&Itemid=
Administers scholarships for Asian Pacific American students.

Scholarships - Nat'l Assoc. of Retired Federal Employees (NARFE)

http://www.feea.org/index.php?option=com_content&task=view&id=17&Itemid=163

Children, stepchildren, and grandchildren of all current NARFE members are eligible to apply for $1,000 college scholarships.

Talbots Women's Scholarship Fund

http://www.talbots.com/about/scholar/scholar.asp?BID=%26h=Mj

Scholarships to women determined to finally get that college degree. Awards are based on financial need & previous achievements for women who earned a HS diploma/GED 10+ years ago.

The Posse Foundation

http://www.possefoundation.org/about-posse/

Recruits and selects student leaders from public high schools to form multicultural teams called "Posses", which go through an intensive college prep program and receive 4-year scholarships.

Truman Scholarship (Harry S. Truman Foundation)

http://www.truman.gov

Awards grants to undergraduate students to attend graduate or professional schools in for a career in government.

Undergraduate Scholarship Program (Natl Institutes of Health)

https://ugsp.nih.gov/home.asp?m=00

Undergraduate Scholarship Program for who are committed to careers in biomedical research.

Undergraduate Scholarships-Morris K. Udall Foundation

http://www.udall.gov/OurPrograms/MKUScholarship/MKUScholarship.aspx

Scholarships to college sophomores & juniors who are committed to environmental careers or are Native Americans committed to careers in tribal public policy or health care.

CHAPTER 15

Student Aid Grants

Unlike loans, grants do not have to be repaid. They are funds provided for eligible students attending colleges and universities. Listed are five notable federal grants.

Academic Competitiveness Grant
http://studentaid.ed.gov/PORTALSWebApp/students/english/
AcademicGrants.jsp
Must be enrolled in a rigorous secondary school.
Annual Award Limit: $976 to $5,350 Up to $750 (first year)
Annual Award Limit: Up to $1,300 (second year)

Federal Pell Grant
http://www.ed.gov/programs/fpg/index.html
Awarded to students who have not earned a bachelor's or graduate degree.
Annual Award Limit: $976 to $5,350

Federal Supplemental Educational Opportunity Grant (FSEOG)
http://www.ed.gov/programs/fseog/index.html
For undergraduates with exceptional financial need.
Annual Award Limit: $200 to $4,000

National Science and Mathematics Access to Retain Talent Grant (National SMART)
http://studentaid.ed.gov/PORTALSWebApp/students/english/
SmartGrants.jsp
Must be enrolled in an eligible degree program majoring in physical, life, or computer sciences, engineering, technology, mathematics, or a critical-need foreign language
Must have a minimum 3.0 cumulative GPA
Annual Award Limit: Up to $4,000

Teacher Education Assistance for College and Higher Education Grant (TEACH)
http://studentaid.ed.gov/PORTALSWebApp/students/english/TEACH.jsp
For undergraduate, post-baccalaureate, or graduate students who are/will be taking course work necessary to become elementary or secondary teachers.
Annual Award Limit: Up to $4,000

CHAPTER 16

Career Path Ideas

Selecting a college major can cause a little anxiety, but it is one of the most important decisions a student must decide upon. It is very common for students to change their major in their sophomore or junior year of college, because the student might experience other interests along the way. Consistent brainstorming for your career path can produce an effective assessment about your future. Mr. Smith had asked himself the following questions during his career discovery, which helped him to identify his direction.

What do I want to do in 20 years?
What are my assignment interests?
What school subjects do I enjoy the most?
What is complicated to others, but yet comes easily for me?

The idea behind selecting a college major is to position your interest, personality and potential into a specific study. Following graduation, many students face a dilemma (especially in our economy today) of finding a job relative to their field of study, but after unsuccessful searches for employment, many of them decide to pursue postgraduate courses and postpone seeking employment. Fortunately, the experiences of attending a college or university provides a positive engagement of development skills needed to be tolerant in adversity such as this. If a student is within reach of acquiring their college degree, then maybe it is now time to narrow the choices for a career path.

Listed below are 10 career path ideas associated with 10 college majors.

No.	Biology Major	Business Management Major	Computer Science Major	Criminal Justice Major	Economics Major
1	Biotechnology	Customer Service Representative	Business Analyst	Administrator of Detectives	Account
2	Clinical Research Associate	Human Resources Assistant	Information Technology Consultant	Attorney	Bank Manager
3	High School Teacher	Human Resources Director	Information Technology Manager	Correctional Officer	Business Analyst
4	Medical Lab Technologist	Human Resources Manager	Information Technology Project Manager	Court Recorder	Controller
5	Medical Research Assistant	Office Manager	Programmer Analyst	Criminal Investigator	Credit Counselor
6	Microbiologist	Operations Manager	Software Architect	Judge	Economics Analyst
7	Pharmacy Technician	Project Manager	Software Developer	Paralegal	Finance Analyst
8	Registered Nurse	Regional Manager	Software Engineer	Police Officer	Finance Consultant
9	Research Lab Technician	Store Assistant Manager	Systems Engineer	Probation Office	Information Technology Manager
10	Veterinarian	Store Manager	Web Developer	Security Guard	Regression/ Statistics Analyst

No.	English Major	History Major	Mechanical Engineering Major	Political Science Major	Psychology Major
1	Administrative Assistant	Attorney	Applications Engineer	Attorney	Clinical Psychologist
2	Copywriter	Grade School Teacher	CAD/CAM Engineer	Educator	Customer Service Representative
3	Executive Administrator	High School Teacher	Mechanical Design Engineer	Government Services	Development Psychologist
4	Grade School Teacher	Librarian	Mechanical Engineer	Journalist	Education Psychologist
5	High School Teacher	Operations Manager	Plant Supervisor	Lecturer	Employment Recruiter
6	Human Resources Manager	Politician	Product Development Engineer	Political Analyst	Human Resources Manager
7	Marketing Director	Professor	Project Engineer	Political Science Instructor	Industrial Organizational Psychologist
8	Office Manager	Publishing Editor	Robotics Engineer	Politician	Mental Health Case Manager
9	Paralegal	Researcher	Senior Engineer	Publisher	Mental Health Counselor
10	Technical Writer	Writer	Structural Designer	Statistical Analyst	Social Worker

Just a note: A person working in a large city or metropolitan area may earn a salary that is considerably more than someone with the same qualifications working in a small city. Workers are often paid salaries that reflect the cost of living in the area where they live and work.

According to an article in Forbes.com by Badenhausen (2008), *"the most lucrative college major today: computer engineering. Those with less than five years' experience are making $60,500, while those with 10 to 20 years' experience are banking $104,000 per year. Today's computer engineering majors are designing the integrated circuits that move information around, and employers like AT&T, Cisco Systems and Hewlett-Packard can't hire enough of them"*.

Listed below is an index of the *Top 20 Popular Lucrative Majors.*
Maybe one of these majors may just interest you.

Table 4		
Top 20 Popular Lucrative College Majors and Projected Employment Pay Scale		
No. 1: Computer Engineering	Experience	Median Salary
	0 to 5 years	$60,500
	5 to 10 years	$80,800
	10 to 20 years	$104,000
No. 2: Economics	Experience	Median Salary
	0 to 5 years	$48,100
	5 to 10 years	$71,800
	10 to 20 years	$96,200
No. 3: Electrical Engineering	Experience	Median Salary
	0 to 5 years	$59,900
	5 to 10 years	$78,400
	10 to 20 years	$96,100
No. 4: Computer Science	Experience	Median Salary
	0 to 5 years	$54,200
	5 to 10 years	$75,100
	10 to 20 years	$94,000
No. 5: Mechanical Engineering	Experience	Median Salary
	0 to 5 years	$56,900
	5 to 10 years	$73,000
	10 to 20 years	$88,100
No. 6: Finance	Experience	Median Salary
	0 to 5 years	$46,900
	5 to 10 years	$64,300
	10 to 20 years	$84,400
No. 7: Mathematics	Experience	Median Salary
	0 to 5 years	$43,500
	5 to 10 years	$64,700
	10 to 20 years	$82,200

No. 8: Civil Engineering	Experience	Median Salary
	0 to 5 years	$52,600
	5 to 10 years	$67,100
	10 to 20 years	$81,700
No. 9: Political Science	Experience	Median Salary
	0 to 5 years	$39,400
	5 to 10 years	$55,000
	10 to 20 years	$74,400
10. Marketing	Experience	Median Salary
	0 to 5 years	$39,400
	5 to 10 years	$54,000
	10 to 20 years	$72,300
11. Accounting	Experience	Median Salary
	0 to 5 years	$44,600
	5 to 10 years	$57,900
	10 to 20 years	$71,500
12. History	Experience	Median Salary
	0 to 5 years	$37,600
	5 to 10 years	$52,100
	10 to 20 years	$68,000
13. Business Management	Experience	Median Salary
	0 to 5 years	$40,900
	5 to 10 years	$51,700
	10 to 20 years	$64,900
14. Communications	Experience	Median Salary
	0 to 5 years	$36,400
	5 to 10 years	$50,300
	10 to 20 years	$64,300
15. English	Experience	Median Salary
	0 to 5 years	$36,700
	5 to 10 years	$47,900
	10 to 20 years	$62,300

16. Biology	Experience	Median Salary
	0 to 5 years	$37,900
	5 to 10 years	$52,600
	10 to 20 years	$60,000
17. Sociology	Experience	Median Salary
	0 to 5 years	$35,700
	5 to 10 years	$46,900
	10 to 20 years	$55,900
18. Graphic Design	Experience	Median Salary
	0 to 5 years	$34,700
	5 to 10 years	$45,300
	10 to 20 years	$54,700
19. Psychology	Experience	Median Salary
	0 to 5 years	$34,700
	5 to 10 years	$45,400
	10 to 20 years	$54,000
20. Criminal Justice	Experience	Median Salary
	0 to 5 years	$34,200
	5 to 10 years	$44,400
	10 to 20 years	$53,400

Source. From "*Most Lucrative College Majors*", by Kurt Badenhausen. Copyright 2010 by Forbes Magazine.

CHAPTER 17

How to Write a Successful Résumé

Many people who have composed a résumé may not realize that they may have written the right résumé for the wrong job, or the wrong résumé for the right job. It is easy to compile your past employment history and qualifications, but do you list the right experiences that are likely to get you that particular job? Always remember that there are blue collar jobs (usually considered physical labor jobs) and white collar jobs (usually considered office-type work), and you should regard each of these categories as different individual positions, to emphasize the skills of the available job. It would be beneficial to compose a résumé for the blue collar jobs and a different résumé for the white collar jobs. **Example:** If you desire a warehouse position at ABC Industries, your résumé information should reflect your past history of shipping and receiving, storage, or inventory labor duties. If you desire a customer service position at ABC Industries, your résumé should reflect your past history of customer assistance practices and any other references that would be an eye-catcher for the employer to see. **NOTE:** Never add fictitious or inaccurate information on your résumé, because most companies will perform a background check to verify the accuracy of your data; if there are discrepancies, the employer most likely will not hire you.

Other résumé writing tips:
- Write a sincere cover letter. Explain why you want to work for their company and why you are the best person for the job. Your cover letter should entice your reader.
- Keep your résumé to a single page, because employers usually spend about ten seconds glancing at a résumé and may not have the time to read multiple pages.
- Do not make your résumé long-winded. Only use relevant information, and try not to be too wordy. The more things you have to say, the more bored your reader may become.
- Use uncomplicated terms when describing an entry. Example: every employer may not know what an *AS/400 machine* is, but if you state

that you worked on the *IBM eServer machine*, then your reader may identify with this device.

- Use bullets to emphasize your important skills. Bullets draw attention to your qualities.
- Use the Times New Roman font style with the twelve font size. This is the standard for "easy-to-read" literature.
- If you receive an interview invitation from an employer, take a longer version of your résumé with you, because your one page résumé may not display all of your qualifications and experiences. You can then present the interviewer with a document that lists all of your knowledge and experience.
- List your e-mail address, home phone number, and cell phone number on your résumé. If the employer cannot reach you at home, then they have two other options to contact you.
- Proofread, proofread, and proofread. Do not rely on a computer spell checker to catch any grammatical errors. Although the spell checker may notice misspelled words, it may not capture the use of alternative words, such as: to, too, or two.
- Fashion your résumé to the job that you are applying for. If you are applying for a computer technician position, you would not want to highlight all of your IT certifications and technical experiences that you performed with previous employers. Emphasize the most relevant tasks that are associated with the position you are applying for.
- List only upstanding and quality references. Some companies may question your listed references and contact them for verification of their relation to you. If there is someone that you feel may hinder your chances for employment, do not list them.

NOTE: Many fired workers may not list the job for which they were terminated on their résumé. You may have to explain the inconsistent time gap in employment when applying for a possible position.

Example:
Blue Collar Résumé

Aubrey Smith

1545 Jacob Street
St. Louis, Missouri 63033
(314) 555-5037
asmith@mye-mail.com

OBJECTIVE

To utilize my 8 years of **warehouse coordinating skills** and to become a valuable Team member.

EMPLOYMENT EXPERIENCE:

ABC Solutions - St. Louis, Missouri   June 2002–Present

Customer Service Manager

- Orders shipping and receiving materials.
- Develops warehouse operational procedures.
- Inspects and performs inventory responsibilities.
- Effectively performs management service requests.

ABC Systems - St. Louis, Missouri   October 2000–June 2002

Regional Manager
- Served as project leader of 18 field technicians.
- Managed day-to-day operations for internal technicians.
- Informed Teammates of all organizational operations and procedures.
- Tracked and immediately resolved the customer's issues.
- Helped to ensure excellent customer service.

SKILLS:

Regional Manager	Restaurant Manager
IT Network Engineer	Shipping and Receiving
Program Management	Customer Service Manager
MSOffice Professional	Professional Business Communicator

EDUCATION:
ABC University, St. Louis, Missouri   BS in Business Administration

---

Example:
White Collar Résumé

Aubrey Smith

1545 Jacob Street
St. Louis, Missouri 63033
(314) 555-5037
asmith@mye-mail.com

OBJECTIVE:

To utilize my 8 years of **customer service and data entry skills** and to become a valuable Team member.

EMPLOYMENT EXPERIENCE:

ABC Solutions - St. Louis, Missouri   June 2002–Present

Customer Service Manager

• Organize specific personnel and customer service issues.
• Develop, implement and maintain company policies and procedures.
• Inspect, compile and maintain each successful customer service requests.
• Effectively acts as a liaison between client and management.

ABC Systems - St. Louis, Missouri   October 2000–June 2002

Regional Manager
• Served as project leader of 18 field technicians.
• Managed day-to-day operations for internal technicians.
• Informed Teammates of all organizational operations and procedures.
• Tracked and immediately resolved the customer's issues.
• Helped to ensure excellent customer service.

SKILLS:

Regional Manager	Restaurant Manager
IT Network Engineer	Shipping and Receiving
Program Management	Customer Service Manager
MSOffice Professional	Professional Business Communicator

EDUCATION:
ABC University, St. Louis, Missouri   BS in Business Administration

CHAPTER 18

Action Words for Your Résumé

Many employers look for key words and phrases on an applicant's résumé. Whenever you are creating or updating your résumé, remember to add the words *team player* or *team leader*, because employers think highly of someone who can work as part of a team environment. The words in **BOLD** lettering are the attention getters.

Accomplished	Convinced	Expanded	Mediated	Repaired
Achieved	Corrected	Explained	Met	Replaced
Acquired	Corresponded	Flagged	Modified	Reported
Adapted	Counseled	Formed	Monitored	Represented
Adjusted	**Created**	Formulated	Motivated	Rescued
Administered	Cultivated	Founded	Negotiated	Researched
Advertised	Debugged	Gathered	Obtained	**Resolved**
Advised	Decreased	Generated	**Operated**	Restored
Analyzed	Delivered	Headed	**Organized**	Reviewed
Appraised	Designated	Hired	Overhauled	Revised
Approved	**Designed**	Honored	Patented	Scheduled
Arbitrated	Detected	Identified	Performed	Screened
Arranged	Determined	Ignited	Persistent	Selected
Assembled	**Developed**	**Implemented**	Persuaded	Self-Starter
Assisted	Devised	Improved	Placed	Served
Attentive	Diagnosed	Increased	Planned	Simplified
Audited	**Directed**	**Influenced**	Posted	Skillful
Authored	Discovered	Initiated	Prepared	Sold
Budgeted	Dispatched	Innovated	Presented	Solved
Built	Distributed	Inspected	Presided	Steered
Calculated	Documented	Installed	Processed	Streamlined
Catalogued	Dynamic	Instituted	**Produced**	Studied

Charted	Edited	Instructed	Professional	Studious
Closed (A Deal)	Elicited	Interpreted	Proficient	Suggested
Coached	Eliminated	Interviewed	Programmed	**Supervised**
Compared	Empowered	**Introduced**	Promoted	Supplied
Compiled	Energetic	**Invented**	Proposed	**Team Leader**
Completed	**Engineered**	Inventoried	Provided	**Team Player**
Composed	**Enhanced**	Justified	Purchased	Tested
Conceptualized	Enterprising	Lectured	Quantified	Tracked
Conducted	Enthusiastic	**Led**	Recognized	Trained
Conscientious	**Established**	Lobbied	Recommended	Transcribed
Consistent	Estimated	Logged	Reconciled	Translated
Consolidated	**Evaluated**	Loyal	**Reduced**	Updated
Constructed	Examined	Maintained	Referred	Utilized
Consulted	Exceeded	Managed	Regulated	Vended
Contacted	Excelled	Manufactured	Reliable	Won
Controlled	Executed	Mastered	Reorganized	Wrote

CHAPTER 19

Preparing for the Employment World

Youthful and seeking employment:
Many employers seek to hire aggressive young adults who are either fresh out of high school or fresh out of college. College students or graduates are seeking something more befitting of their education or field of study. Some of the entry-level positions at fast-food restaurants, grocery stores, or service stations, are designed for the recent high school graduate, but there are many adults in their twenties that may seek these positions also.

Several tips that can assist with your employment search are:
- Dress for the position, and for the employer. You would not wear an apron and hairnet to an interview for a construction position. Khakis, a nice dress shirt, and soft-soled shoes would be more appropriate.
- If you acquire the job that you are seeking, do not consider the position as a temporary position or a "stepping-stone". Do not treat your new position as though it is just there until something better comes along. When you secretly or publically display this attitude, you will make it more difficult for yourself to stay motivated to work there.
- Do not take the attitude that you are better than the job you are doing. Remember, your current position will be on your future résumé, and future employers may question your work experience on that job. It is better to do your best.
- Entry-level positions have a higher turnover rate, because of the modest skills needed to perform the required tasks. It would be wise to do your best and acquire as much training as possible, because you may need this experience later in life.

Middle-aged and seeking employment:
Today's downturn in the economy is what many call a "Great Depression *Recession*". This time in history will have an impact on our generation the same way that our parents and grandparents were affected by the same types of situations. Middle-aged and older people who have been without

a steady-paying job for quite sometime are anxious to return to the working environment because of their dwindling savings account, lack of healthcare benefits, or just for the active surroundings. However, an employer may covertly discriminate against the applicant and hold out for a younger applicant. Be aware of some employers' stereotypical mindset that a person who is half the age of an applicant may be twice as productive, or an employer may side with the younger applicant because of their naïve ways and willingness to do whatever it takes to succeed.

Several ways that can assist with your employment pursuit is to:
- During interviews, be as cordial as you can be with remarks of "yes sir" or "no ma'am", even if you are the oldest person in the room. By displaying respect to the interviewer (regardless of his age), you allow them to sense mutual reverence and appreciation.
- Limit recording outdated experiences on your résumé. Be cautious of specifying old graduation dates or other dates of long-ago on your résumé. This can be a dead give-away of your age.
- Get familiar with the new technology terminology. Bear in mind that there is so much technology in the workforce that no one person knows it all, but prior to an interview, it would be beneficial to you to investigate what type of technology that the company requires their employees to know.

Remember, the employer has certain preferences and interests that the company desires for the applicant to possess. It may be predetermined as to the type of candidate that is needed for the position, so do not be discouraged or get disheartened because you did not acquire the job. If you are successful with getting an interview with a company, then you can be even more successful with your next interview, because now you have interviewing experience. We will not get every job that we apply for.

CHAPTER 20

Interviewing Etiquette

Congratulations, your résumé was successful, because an employer enjoyed your input and contacted you. Now what do you do? Research and prepare. Mrs. Smith and I have compiled a few points of etiquette and some interviewing questions and answers that we have encountered during some of our interviews. We have interviewed for many jobs and have made many mistakes along the way. Through experience, we have learned what works and what doesn't work to land a job. From an employer perspective, I have interviewed hundreds of applicants over the years, and some of the responses that I have received were quite out of the ordinary. The key to an impressive interview is to try and remain calm, be yourself (easier said than done), focus on your employment objective, and visualize that you are there to display your skills. Another very important tip is to research the company you are interviewing with, by learning their history, financial status, and other outstanding details. This could be your future employer, so be impressive. Possibly the best person that I had the pleasure of interviewing was the candidate who sat in the interview and quoted our company's mission statement and Quarterly Financial Reports; and he was also aware of the company's upper-management team. This candidate used his local career center library and did research on the Internet about our company. I was so impressed with his job skills, people skills, and interviewing skills that he was hired on the spot.
Lastly, send a follow-up letter or a follow-up e-mail after every interview. Believe me; this makes a very good impression with the interviewer. Listed below are some helpful points regarding interviewing conduct and etiquette and a few of my favorite responses to interview questions.

Good interviewing behavior begins with practice and determination to succeed and (ultimately) getting hired. The following suggestions can assist you with a successful interview:

- **Research the company, the position, and, if possible, the people (or person) who will conduct your interview:** You want to know all about the company that may eventually hire you, and by displaying your knowledge of the company to the interviewer, you may be the proactive person that the company is seeking.

- **Dress appropriately:** Before arriving for the interview, inquire about the required dress code, because you would not want to wear a wedding dress to a receptionist interview or a three-piece suit to an interview for a fry cook position at a fast food restaurant. A white conventional shirt or blouse is more appropriate. Many employers will despise visible body piercings (eyebrow rings, nose rings, etc). It is important to dress to fit the company and the job.

- **Professional care:** Your perfume, cologne, or makeup should not "speak too loudly", and be sure that your breath is not offensive when speaking to the interviewer.

- **Arrive on time:** Leave home early enough to arrive to the interview on time. Do not arrive more than thirty minutes early. By arriving early, you display promptness and eagerness to meet for the interview.

- **Sound check:** Prior to meeting the interviewer, turn off your cell phone, pager, or any other electronic device that may interrupt your interview.

- **Saying "Hello":** Introduce yourself to the interviewer; pronounce his name correctly, and greet him with a firm handshake.

- **Taking a seat:** Do not sit down until you are asked to take a seat, and use good posture.

- **Coffee? Soft drink?** If offered a cup of coffee, soft drinks, or any other beverage, try not to accept it (unless you are at an interview meal or you need a beverage to quench your thirst). If you do accept a drink, where would you put the beverage? On the floor, on your lap, or on the interviewers desk? It would be inappropriate to hold the drink during your entire interview, because you will need both hands free (to present additional documentation, shake hands or just for the independence). Another problem with holding a beverage could be, if you spill the beverage during the interview, you may spill your chances for an exceptional interview, and possibly the position. Do not eat, drink, or chew gum during your interview, because this is not a social occasion; this is an interview for your future.

- **Updated résumé and documentation:** Present to the interviewer an expanded résumé and other credentials which display additional work experiences.

- **Be observant:** During the interview, relax, but stay alert, and display strong interest in the position. Maintain eye contact when speaking to the interviewer.

- **Smile:** This is an expression denoting pleasure and appreciation for the interview.
- **Your dialogue:** Keep your conversation short. An interviewer does not want to hear your life story.
- **Appropriate language:** Do not use profanity of any kind. An interviewer may feel threatened with your choice of words, and he may also feel that you are not the right person for the company's ethical environment.
- **Honesty:** Do not lie about your job experience, education, or anything that is related to your past or current work history. Be truthful in everything that you say.
- **Conversation approach:** Present positive points of view and an optimistic attitude when speaking about the position. Avoid any negative comments about any past employers or past employees.
- **Salary inquiry:** Avoid asking about the salary, because you should already have an idea of what the position pays. The salary is one of the reasons that you agreed to attend the interview.
- **Sharing contact information:** Be sure to acquire a business card from the interviewer, and if you have a card, it would be favorable to leave one of your cards upon completion of your interview.
- **Saying "Good-bye":** Exit the interview with a firm handshake, and thank the interviewer for their time.
- **Express gratitude:** Immediately following your interview (if you have Internet access), send a "thank-you" e-mail or letter to the interviewer. If you wait until you arrive home, it is appropriate to send a thank-you note within twenty-four hours, and reassert how interested you are in the position.

Things to Remember:
- The interviewer has already read your résumé, so be prepared to explain any information listed, and do not supply any vague answers (or incomplete responses).
- By being impressive in your interview, you may be asked to attend a second or third interview; this is why your first interview must be flawless.
- Your body language is being examined, so do not play with your hair or with items in your pockets.
- Do not cut your interview short because of another appointment. Dedicate each interview as though it is your only appointment for that day.

- Perform your interview as though the employer needs you more than you need them.
- It may take several weeks before you hear from the employer. Try to be patient, and stay optimistic.
- Do not become too informal with the interviewer by calling him by his first name, unless the interviewer insists that you do so.
- When completing your application, be sure that it is legible and complete.
- Do not call the interviewer without permission to inquire about the hiring development of the position.
- After completing an interview, be prepared to attend the next one, by repeating the above actions.

CHAPTER 21

Interviewing Questions and Answers

In most of your interviews, you will hear questions that are unexpected and surprising. Be attentive and alert, and as the saying goes, "expect the unexpected". Some of the following questions are basic statements that may be asked during an interview and below each question are we our supporting answers that are relevant to the question.

Tell me about yourself?
"I am reliable, hard working, and an excellent team-oriented person. My current goal is to continue my education".

What do you know about our company?
"From your Web site and other media research, I have discovered that your mission statement reflects your company's excellent reputation".

Why are you interested in this position?
"With my work ethic, experience, and education, I believe that I would be a great fit to your team".

What is your greatest weakness?
"Sometimes I can be a perfectionist and focus too much on being a detail-oriented employee".

How do you work under pressure?
"Very well; I can confront and take control of a challenge."

Can you tell me about your plans for the future?
"My goal is to become an excellent teammate with your company and to continue my education."

What salary are you worth?
"Top pay in this department, because I believe that I am very qualified for the position."

Would your last employer recommend you?
"Yes, very highly."

How do you feel about performing routine work?
"I am certain that I would be very productive, and I would gladly accept the challenge."

How do you get along with other people?
"Excellent; I enjoy team-work."

What can you tell me about yourself, which shows that you have initiative?
"My decision-making experience has taught me how to focus on the most important issues and to quickly make ethical conclusions. Most decisions require only a yes-or-no answer, and I regularly present a reason why I selected *yes* or *no*."

What does it take for a company to become successful?
"I believe that it takes teamwork, reliability, and hard work from each employee."

What do your former coworkers think of you?
"They recognize that I have an excellent work record and that I will perform an assignment correctly."

As a leader, how approachable are you?
"My daily goal is to continue to fully serve each customer with high quality individual and business services."

What can your customers speak about you?
"My relationship with our customers is on a semi-personal level, and we exchange social greetings. Each of our most frequent customers has my cell phone number, and they do contact me whenever there is a need for immediate assistance."

How is your knowledge of your previous employer's policies and practices?
"I fully understood the current policies for both the customer side and the internal side of the business. I developed my skills through the company training courses that are offered by our Human Resources Department."

When leading a group, how will you face difficult times?
"I continue to stay focused on the current situation, and then make wise decisions shortly afterwards. My attitude and stress levels remain consistent."

Can you describe a management conflict that you were involved in?
"When there was a difference in work ethic between one of our customers and a technician that I managed, I immediately contacted that customer and discussed the dispute; I then contacted the technician involved to listen to their report. After quickly establishing a resolution, the customer was contacted with the update. The customer approved the resolution decision, and it was quickly resolved."

Can you tell me about your customer focus?
"Listening to and understanding our customer is the best way to provide exactly what they are looking for. I have always displayed courteous conduct and a respectful behavior, and I provide immediate assistance to each customer."

What is your decision-making process?
"My daily business focus is on disciplined thinking, as I reflect on all of the positive and negative effects that my decisions can bring. My course of action is: analyzing the issue, surveying all persons and materials involved, concentrating on the facts, timely responsiveness, and my final action—the decision."

How well do you direct and motivate subordinates?
"The guidelines that I provide to the team are the procedures that have been established by our company, but the values that I communicate to them are based on continuance of high-quality performances. My motivating processes are directed at influencing a person's behavior so that they can perform as expected."

What was considered to be a very challenging issue as a leader?
"The elimination of the use of profanity by our employees while in the company of a customer. Eliminating foul language displays moral ethics and verbal respect to the customer."

What principles did you instruct as a leader?
"The directions that I forwarded to each employee were the business objectives created by the company."

How strong was your confidence when facing a problematic employee?
"I practiced good managerial courage by presenting an equal, fair, and open-minded reaction to an employee's point of view during a disciplinary moment. I did not substitute friendly, kind words for firm criticism when the occasion called for critical feedback."

What was your primary goal as a leader?
"My most important priority was to serve our clients, but also inspire our team to produce a smooth-running operation."

What is your process management approach?
"My process management approach is a very effective business flowchart. I continually strive to improve the services and operations that comply with the requests of the customer."

What is your most efficient management quality?
"My awareness of quality is centered on the customer. My employer designed a vision for a significant level of customer excellence, and I have followed and passed this concept on to team members to improve our customer relationships."

Why should we hire you?
"Because I am very qualified for the position."

What qualifications do you have?
"I have letters of recognition, job certifications, and performance awards."

How many other companies have you approached?
"Very few, but your company is my primary objective."

What did you like and dislike about your last job?
Like: "All of my coworkers."

Dislike: "My computer was too slow."

How has your previous job helped prepare you for our available position?
"The knowledge has provided me with hands-on skill. I believe that I can add value to your team by sharing my experience."

Did you ever have a disagreement with your manager?
"No, because we had a great working relationship."

In your lifetime, what has been your greatest employment accomplishment?
"The opportunity I have right now, to meet you for the interview with your company."

In your lifetime, what has been your greatest employment failure?
"I missed out on my perfect-attendance award by only two days."

What was your worst disappointment?
"I was overlooked for a position that I was qualified for. Even though the person hired for the position was the best choice for the company, I did not display resentment toward the company or the other candidate; we actually became great coworkers and friends)."

If hired, when do you expect to leave this company?
"If I was hired by your company, I would hope to stay until retirement age."

Are you at your best when working with a group or working alone?
"I enjoy working both, but I am best when leading a team."

Give me a reason why I should not hire you?
"There are no reasons, because I am the best candidate for the position."

What do you like most about yourself?
"I feel that I am trustworthy, and my coworkers depend on me to properly accomplish a task."

Describe the type of person that you think would do well in our company?
"I believe that it takes a self-starting motivator."

How do you know that you are capable of handling this position?
"Because of my professional training and experience."

Where does this job fit in with your career goals?
"This position is my career goal."

Do you have any questions for me?
"Yes, I do." **(See chapter 22: Questions to Ask the Interviewer)**

Inappropriate Questions that the interviewer should not ask you
There are various state and federal laws that prohibit employers from requesting certain information about an applicant. Sometimes specific questions can be aimed toward discrimination, which could suppress your hiring status. Although you are entitled to not answer any of the questions below, you can state to the interviewer that the question is improper.

- How old are you?
- What is your height?
- What is your weight?
- Are you a U.S. citizen?
- When did you graduate?
- Do you have a disability?
- What is your nationality?
- Do you have any children?
- What is your marital status?
- Are you a man or a woman?
- Have you ever been arrested?
- Do you use alcohol or smoke?
- Do you prefer Miss, Mrs. or Ms?
- What is your religious affiliation?
- How long have you lived in the United States?

CHAPTER 22

Questions to Ask the Interviewer

Now it is your turn to interview your potential employer. Remember, you do not have to ask basic questions, such as *"What is the title of this position?"* or *"What does the position pay?"* because you should already know this information prior to your interview. Try to keep your questions short, and above all:

a) **Do not pressure the interviewer with your questioning.** The interviewer may be working under a short timeline for your interview, and there may be other applicants that he is scheduled to interview.

b) **Always display respect when asking and responding to every question.** The interviewer may form a high opinion of you when you acknowledge him in this regard.

c) **Observe the interviewer's body language. If the interviewer is becoming annoyed or impatient, end your interview questions and thank him for his input.** It is important to recognize if the interviewer displays signs that the interview should be over; show consideration and immediately close your interview questioning.

Below are ten informational questions that can give you more insight of the employer.

1. Why is this position open?
2. How often are merits awarded?
3. Will there be room for advancement?
4. What past issues were there with this position?
5. What are the expected work hours for this position?
6. Does the company participate in college reimbursement?
7. What significant company changes are in the near future?
8. Who would be my direct and indirect contact for support?
9. How often has this position been filled in the past five years?
10. How soon will the company make a decision to fill the position?

CHAPTER 23

Ways to Maintain Your Current Job

Now that you have landed your new job, you want to hold on to it! The days of working for the same employer for thirty years have passed. Your coworkers and managers can be highly impressed with just your team-player potential. Mrs. Smith and I have compiled a list of our managerial experiences and a few quality methods that can help you establish a good reputation and protect your status while on the job.

Do not try to outshine your coworkers:
When you surpass or outclass your coworkers intentionally and in an insensitive manner, you may be viewed as a nonteam player. You do not want to be targeted as someone who betrays their coworkers. I witnessed a coworker who had become a "show-off" by excelling and surpassing fellow coworkers with job duties, but in an inconsiderate and mean-spirited way. After several counseling sessions, accompanied by our Human Resources department, the employee still believed that his actions were for the good of the company. Shortly thereafter, Human Resources received the employee's resignation. Believing that his coworkers were jealous, he felt unappreciated and walked away from a good-paying job.

Always do your best with your job:
Do not be complacent, relaxed, or careless, when performing your duties, and always do your best to execute efficiently. Managers are inspired when an employee has achieved a personal best or when they have completed a difficult task while on the job. Just because you may not receive credit for the accomplishment, it does not mean that your coworkers are not affected by your performance.

Develop your skills:
You can progress and enhance your chances of staying on-board with your employer by improving your performance and going the "extra mile" to increase your job knowledge. Mrs. Smith and I are continually learning how to improve our efficiency and understanding of our current jobs, which will allow us to properly prepare for our next employment goal.

Keep your promises:
If a coworker or manager requests assistance, and you offer to lend a hand, make sure that you follow through on your promise. When you do not keep your word, your teammates will lose trust in you. As a manager, one of my utmost annoyances is when a teammate assures me that he will undertake a task for me but fails to complete it. If there are issues out of his control that hinder him from keeping his promise, then I can sympathize; but, if he still shows all the signs of guaranteeing the promise but fails to get around to completing the task, then it would be difficult for me to trust him for any special assignments in the near future.

Do not complain about company policies and procedures:
Sometimes it may be difficult to not say anything when your strategy and that of the company differ. Business guidelines are in place to support the employees and the company; but if there are unsafe practices or any procedures that can improve the productivity of the company, then management would be most interested in hearing them.

Watch out for that "trusting" individual:
Be cautious about who you confide in with your problems and concerns, and when and where you express them. Sometimes the "open door policy" may be a silent screening to identify the whistle blowers—so be cautious of whom you trust.

Do not become a know-it-all:
It is usually acceptable to be a clever person who knows many things, but your coworkers may avoid you if they sense that you are a person who feels that they know everything about everything. Do not be the person that relentlessly corrects the analysis and opinions of others. Managers respect and admire those who are smart, but there is very little honor for those who are a smart-aleck.

Stay positive, motivated and be happy to have a job:
Our national economic situation has stretched our financial system very thin. There are thousands of workers that would be happy to have your job. If demotions or pay cuts are offered, immediately accept them, and then test the job market for a better-paying position. Remember, money isn't everything, but job security and benefits, along with the paycheck, should be the motivation you need to stay positive.

Do not become disloyal to your coworkers:
It is better to fit in with your coworkers than to be the person who leans

toward management's side of an issue, abandoning your teammates in the process. Siding with management to improve quality is encouraged, but do not agree with your coworkers and then inform management that you disagree with your coworkers. You want to maintain your coworkers' and manager's personal confidence in you.

Do not distribute gossip:
Spreading idle talk and gossip can classify you as troublemaker. Some rumors can cause disorder among the team. Management may be well aware of those who gossip or spread rumors, and this type of behavior reflect poorly on the employee.

Stay well-groomed and neatly dressed:
A pleasant and well-groomed employee is what the company wants to present to their customers. Most employers have a dress code, and it would be dutiful to comply with those regulations.

Always arrive to work on time:
Entering the workplace late or missing a deadline, due to tardiness, is a job killer. If your employer suggests that you stay after work to make up for lost work time, be compliant. One of the managers in my workplace has an office located near the main aisle, which everyone must take to get to their work station. This manager has a direct view of employees as they arrive at work in the morning, and he would know if anyone arrived late. It would be beneficial to always arrive at work on time, because it may be documented as to how many times you have been late for work.

Keep your work area neat:
Try to maintain a business atmosphere. Too many family snapshots and personal belongings displayed around your work area may be viewed as a personal atmosphere and not a business environment. I encourage teammates to limit pictures of their loved ones and to develop a paper-management system, to prevent clutter. These can be distractions to the teammate and to any visiting customers.

Admit your mistakes:
Displaying dishonesty or trying to devise a plan to side-step an issue when you were at fault, may turn your coworkers against you. Acknowledge your errors, and graciously accept the responsibility. Managers are aware that mistakes are all part of operating a business. Although unintentional mistakes are the ones that prompt managers to improve internal processes, it is the intentional maneuvers that cause employees to lose their jobs. I

once managed an employee who was color-blind, but he never informed anyone on the team of this. His job duties required him to identify and verify certain colors of cabling and wires. During his first assignment, he informed me that he could not tell the difference in the wiring schemes. Not long after, he was dismissed from employment for not being truthful by revealing his inability to distinguish colors.

Do not reply to personal e-mail while at work:
If it is not a business message, then replying to the e-mail should be done away from work. Many companies may not allow unsolicited e-mail accounts to penetrate the company firewall, and the company has the right to intercept any message that travels through their network. Another objectionable communication practice that managers are opposed to is the jokes, comical stories, and nonbusiness-related messages that are distributed internally throughout a company. Refrain from replying to or forwarding these types of messages.

Never be deceitful:
Never take credit for someone else's efforts. Not only are you accepting undeserved recognition, but you will make many enemies when doing so. Honesty in the workplace is an ongoing challenge, but when you observe this principle, perhaps your coworkers will follow your example.

Recognize your abilities:
If you are unfamiliar with an assignment, ask questions on how to complete the task. Do not assume that you know how to fulfill the request, because you may be jeopardizing the whole project. Managers are strategically placed within an organization to assist employees with issues and to offer training to enhance their abilities. Asking for assistance does not reduce your status with management. It is better to ask for help than to ask for forgiveness.

Keep clear of interoffice romantic relationships:
This can ruin a career. It is easy to form a relationship with someone that you work with on a daily basis, but try to keep it professional and not romantic. A committed work romance may affect your work ethic and performance.

Enhance your priorities:
By sustaining a well-adjusted and objective presence, you may discover more lucrative ways to resolve on-the-job issues. Managers are continually trying to increase employee productivity, improve company results, and develop

the entire team professionally, as each of these benefits the organization. An employee who can flourish with managing their priorities is a very successful employee.

Readjust your improper work practices:
Try to alter and fine-tune any inappropriate actions while at work, such as: poor task planning, a messy desk, or placing personal life before work. An unbalanced work routine can affect the entire team, and your manager and coworkers may not appreciate any of these actions. Remember, if anything is obstructing your goals, then it should be removed.

Stay clear of the circle of unprincipled individuals:
The company that you keep at work may eventually affect your personal life,and. you may regret it. Do not be influenced by others who practice unprofessional methods.

Responding to completed responsibilities:
When asked about the status of your assignments, try to respond with an explanation of the level of completion, instead of a simple yes or no. Your manager will appreciate input on what contributed to your success or what prevented you from completing your assignments.

Remain completely competent and flexible:
Always use logical decisions when performing your job duties. *Managers observe and examine employee competence, job performance, and assessment methods, and verify the level of productivity.*

Speak clearly and understandably:
When communicating with managers and coworkers, it is essential to communicate in a clear, relaxed, and effective manner.

Recognize the value of your support team:
Learn how to appreciate your coworkers and managers, and make sure you understand the direction of your team's goal. Creating a supportive work environment helps eliminate negative stress and work overload.

For Leaders and Managers:
I believe that the difference between a manager and a leader is; Management is a professional career and Leadership is a calling. A manager directs team members to ensure that each member is carrying out their assignments according to company procedures. If there is an issue within the company, a good manager solves the issue, isolates it and assures that the issue will not reoccur. A leader is the person who guides their team toward a common

goal by leading as an example, but most importantly, a leader must be fully trusted by the team. When you appropriately combine the two roles, the business enterprise will flourish. Before becoming a regional manager, I was taught to give employees credit when and where credit was due. This principle is a valuable relationship builder. Being perceptive of the team's needs and displaying appreciation to each member goes a long way with producing trust and acceptance. Some advice that I would like to share with other managers is to; trust in your team and display your leadership. When ideal team members are in place, and each of them is proficient with the company's processes, then allowing them to perform their expected duties is what they were hired to do. When leading your team, and if at all possible, try to stay clear of micromanagement; if the team is following procedures and is very productive, closely observing their every move can lead to employees not fully demonstrating their creative capabilities.

CHAPTER 24

On-the-Job-Challenges: Things Not to Get Discouraged About While at Work

There are many other applicants that are looking for a job like yours. Keeping a level mind and positive attitude can be encouraging to you and your coworkers. There are no perfect jobs, nor are there perfect employees. Being rejected by coworkers occurs at most companies. If you are so unhappy about how your coworkers treat you and you resign from that job, remember: there may be a worse group of coworkers on your next job.

The following circumstances can occur in any job situation, some of which Mrs. Smith and I have encountered during our employment careers:

Not having a college degree or a lesser degree than the college graduates that you work with on a daily basis:
Do not feel that you are at a disadvantage, because approximately thirty percent of Americans have a college degree; besides, it's never too late to acquire one.

Being a minority employee among nonminority coworkers:
Stay optimistic, because no matter what your heritage is, you are there to accomplish a goal. Interactions with your coworkers display your diversity leadership.

Being scrutinized as a minority for possessing a job title above a nonminority:
This is a great opportunity to truly stand out and provide evidence that you are the proper person for the job. Remember, there are laws against discrimination in the workplace.

Being scorned for possessing a job that one of your coworkers feels that one of their family members should have:
You were selected for the job because of your skills, so do not allow a coworker to suppress you. It could affect your work performance.

Be disrespected for possessing a job title above friends (who happen to be your coworkers):
By staying in control and understanding how to separate friendship and business, they may take notice and follow your authority.

Being a Christian in the workplace:
Although discussion of religion is frowned upon within the workplace, displaying a Christian attitude by being an honest, trustworthy person may help you receive a promotion.

Being one of the oldest or youngest employees in the company:
Feel privileged to be the "baby" in the company or even the "elder statesman." It may have not been an easy mission in acquiring your position, so regardless of your age, it should be an honor to be an employee at any company.

Feeling left out of certain inner circles:
You are not at work to join intimate groups, only to perform professionally. Some internal cliques are on a professional level.

Being the target of racial or religious jokes:
Sometimes the best remedy for this problem is a direct approach. Be cordial, and speak to your coworker in private. You can say to your coworker that you do not appreciate the jokes, and to please cease telling them immediately.

Placed with excessive duties and responsibilities when other coworkers with the same job title have lesser duties:
This could be a test from management, to observe your responsiveness and attitude. If the work gets too overwhelming, then it would be wise to ask for help.

Not receiving the same respect and accolades as other coworkers:
Sometimes it is difficult to come within reach of a goal or award and not attain it, but try not to focus too much on the loss. Create a different goal. Remember, you may not receive respect from every coworker, although compliments and admiration are always welcomed. Stay confident and assertive, because your day will arrive soon.

Feeling that you are expected to do more of the unpleasant tasks than all of your coworkers because you do not have a college degree (or higher education) than other coworkers:
Do not consider this as an attack on your education or character. There are some coworkers who may feel that they are above you socially and may take advantage of you. By taking the liberty to perform the additional duties, you may be considered by management to be a more reliable and efficient employee.

Being left out of many group discussions and personal conversations:
This should not be a big problem, because if you are not included in those conversations, management will notice that you are working while others are talking.

Not being invited to after-hours functions:
You could be wasting time and money by attending certain functions. Be wise to the entertainment, costs, and purpose for attending.

Only spoken to when a coworker is in need of something work–related:
This should tell you how reliable you are with your job duties, and your coworkers consider you as the *go-to* person. Do not be discouraged about not being approached with personal conversation, because you work for the company, not for the individual.

Given responsibilities at work that other coworkers do not want to perform:
Sometimes being the easy target can wear on you. If the situation gets worse, talk to your boss.

Having a position that hires new employees (based on applicants' experience and not their race), but being scrutinized by upper management for hiring a minority:
By adhering to the policies and procedures of the company, there should not be any repercussions for doing your job.

Being patronized or given lack of respect for who you are as a person:
Remember, everyone has their flaws, and no one is perfect, but when you receive unwanted attention, then it may be harassment. The most important thing to do is to peacefully ask the person committing the act to discontinue the harassment. If the person continues, immediately inform the Human Resources department or your manager.

Feeling that you only have your job because of the "ten percent required minority standard":
Even if you feel this way, believe that you were hired because you were the right person for the job. You were placed there for a reason.

For hearing the occasional racial food remark (fried chicken, tacos, fried rice) or any other variety of ethnic cuisine:
Do not be disheartened by any of these (or any other comments), because when the work day is done, most of your coworkers who make these comments may eat the same dishes that they joked to you about.

The occasional "slip of the tongue" racial or religious remark:
Most everyone is consciously aware of what they are preparing to say, so a "slip of the tongue" remark may be a premeditated statement. Remember the old saying "sticks and stones….". Regardless if the remark was stated in jest or an accident, do not let this discourage you. You do have an option (and right) to confront the issue, but if you do report it, it should be performed quietly and confidentially.

Coworkers quickly assume that you are the culprit of missing office items:
Although everyone cannot possess a "clean-cut" image, one of the best ways to avoid any blame is to always display a trustworthy quality. Your behavior can convince others of your unquestionable honesty.

Being undercut for promotions:
Stay encouraged and continue with your work ethic, because you are being noticed and observed as a reliable employee. Your advancement day may be sooner than you can imagine.

Feeling unappreciated for not having a college degree:
You do not have to have a college degree to be a successful person. There have been nine U.S. presidents that did not graduate from college; and possibly our greatest president, Abraham Lincoln, was a lawyer before becoming president.

At the beginning of every work day, you feel that your coworkers will ridicule or annoy you for not conforming to their standards or for making you feel that you are not doing a "good enough job":
You are there to perform for the company and to provide for your family. No employee should ever feel that there is a "guilt-trip" cloud hanging over their head. There is no need for a remorseful feeling when serving

the company with your hard work and long hours while others are there to belittle you.

Consistently hearing profanity at work when each of your coworkers is aware that you do not submit or condone the use of foul language:
Possibly the best way to handle this is to "just walk away". If any of your coworkers continue to display disrespect toward you, you can inform them privately and request that they discontinue the use of profanity when you are in their presence. There are no laws for profanity in the workplace, but if the words are directed toward a particular group (like race, sex, or religion), then it can be considered harassment.

Not receiving full assistance from coworkers when assistance is needed:
Although it may be a little difficult to perform a duty alone, when help is needed, always ask a coworker and a manager for assistance.

Not receiving the workday greeting from coworkers:
When you receive a greeting from a coworker, you gather a warm welcome that can remain with you throughout the workday, but when you do not receive a greeting, it can ruin your day. Do not exhibit displeasure because it can lead to an undesirable exchange of words. You can certainly believe that your coworker is well aware of their inappropriate action.

CHAPTER 25

The Best 50 Jobs in America

Mrs. Smith and I have worked several jobs where we felt overworked and overwhelmed, and during these times, we discussed the venture of a career change. Well this is not an overnight process, and we knew the potential risks of discontinuing one profession and beginning another. Our course of action was to become more educated in the field that we were truly interested in and one that would benefit our family. After we were able to discover a step-by-step plan of selecting a stimulating new career, things became so clear and easy, which made it uncomplicated for us to pursue a different occupation. It's not always about the "top paying job" that fulfills or embraces a successful career, but as we have experienced, it takes an inclusive setting to formulate a satisfying career. Settings such as: job security, minimal job pressures, a job with a meaningful purpose and of course, good pay with adequate employee benefits.

Listed below is an astonishing chart that displays how to choose an ideal employment opportunity.

Table 5

A Ranked Comparison of the Best 50 Jobs in America

Legend for chart:
A: MEDIAN EXPERIENCED PAY
B: TOP PAY
C: 10-YEAR GROWTH RATE
D: TOTAL CURRENT EMPLOYMENT
E: FLEXIBILITY
F: BENEFIT TO SOCIETY
G: PERSONAL SATISFACTION
H: STRESS

Rank	Position	A	B	C	D	E	F	G	H
1	Systems Engineer	$87,100	$130,000	45%	88,000	A	C	A	C
2	Physician Assistant	$90,900	$124,000	27%	82,000	B	A	A	C
3	College Professor	$70,400	$115,000	23%	278,000	A	A	A	B
4	Nurse Practitioner	$85,200	$113,000	23%	23,000	B	A	A	D
5	IT Project Manager	$98,700	$140,000	16%	174,000	A	C	B	C
6	Certified Public Accountant	$74,200	$138,000	18%	189,000	B	C	B	C
7	Physical Therapist	$74,300	$98,100	27%	181,000	B	A	A	C
8	Computer Security Consultant	$99,700	$152,000	27%	13,000	B	B	A	C
9	Intelligence Analyst	$82,500	$115,000	15%	51,000	B	A	A	C
10	Sales Director	$140,000	$239,000	10%	97,000	A	B	B	C
11	Anesthesiologist	$292,000	$408,000	14%	23,000	B	A	A	D
12	Software Developer	$79,400	$116,000	28%	796,000	A	C	B	B
13	Pharmacist	$109,000	$134,000	22%	198,000	B	A	B	C
14	Occupational Therapist	$69,700	$100,000	23%	107,000	B	A	A	C
15	Nurse Anesthetist	$157,000	$214,000	23%	19,000	B	A	A	D
16	Software Product Manager	$106,000	$148,000	28%	37,000	A	C	A	C
17	IT Business Analyst	$82,600	$119,000	29%	125,000	B	C	B	C
18	Attorney	$115,000	$262,000	11%	541,100	B	B	B	C
19	Physician/General Practice	$150,000	$228,000	14%	90,000	B	A	A	D
20	Human Resources Manager	$71,800	$111,000	13%	226,000	B	B	A	C
21	Financial Analyst	$79,900	$109,000	34%	127,000	B	C	B	C
22	Physician/OB-GYN	$222,000	$338,000	14%	14,000	B	A	A	C
23	Clinical Psychologist	$81,100	$172,000	16%	57,000	B	A	A	C
24	Psychiatrist	$177,000	$279,000	14%	20,000	B	A	A	D
25	Veterinarian	$83,900	$157,000	35%	68,000	B	A	B	D
26	Marketing Manager	$76,600	$126,000	14%	138,000	B	C	B	C
27	Speech/Language Pathologist	$70,900	$116,000	11%	113,000	B	A	B	C

28	Technical Writer	$67,400	$99,600	20%	84,000	B B B B
29	Finance Director	$121,000	$214,000	13%	59,000	B B B C
30	Telecom Network Engineer	$86,200	$130,000	53%	21,000	B B B B
31	Director of Communications	$78,300	$135,000	17%	26,000	A B A C
32	Hotel General Manager	$76,800	$146,000	12%	121,000	A B B C
33	Securities Trader	$113,000	$491,000	25%	17,000	B C B C
34	Account Executive	$81,400	$157,000	10%	76,000	B C B C
35	Education Training Consultant	$77,800	$157,000	22%	23,000	B B A B
36	Corporate Paralegal	$65,600	$96,000	22%	40,000	A C B B
37	Quality-Control Engineer	$69,300	$96,800	45%	27,000	B B A C
38	Manufacturing Engineer	$75,100	$103,000	20%	149,000	B B B C
39	Software Program Manager	$110,000	$152,000	28%	11,000	A B B D
40	Applications Systems Analyst	$71,500	$95,900	29%	14,000	A C A C
41	Senior Internal Auditor	$75,500	$106,000	18%	42,000	A C B B
42	Commercial Property Manager	$75,400	$123,000	15%	35,000	A C A C
43	Creative Director	$86,900	$157,000	26%	29,000	A C A C
44	Pharmaceuticals Sales Rep	$105,000	$138,000	12%	61,000	A B B C
45	Investment Banking Associate	$106,000	$221,000	34%	13,000	B C B D
46	Training and Development Manager	$86,900	$120,000	16%	30,000	A B A C
47	Product Marketing Manager	$105,000	$146,000	14%	38,000	A B B D
48	Quality-Assurance Manager	$79,500	$122,000	16%	51,000	A B B D
49	Financial Research Analyst	$65,500	$155,000	34%	18,000	A C B C
50	Outside Sales Representative	$66,900	$125,000	12%	72,000	A C B C

Notes: All pay data from PayScale.com. Median pay is for an experienced worker (at least two to seven years in field). Top pay represents the 90th percentile. Job growth is estimated for 2006-16. Total current employment level is estimated number of people working in each specific job.

Source. From *"The 50 Best Jobs in America"*, by Money/Payscale.com. Copyright 2009 by Money Magazine.

References:

Badenhausen, K. (2008). Forbes.com. *Most Lucrative College Majors*. Retrieved from http://www.forbes.com/2008/06/18/college-majors-lucrative-lead-cx_kb_0618majors_slide_2.html?partner=abcnews

Bureau of Labor Statistics. (2010). *Employed and unemployed persons by occupation*. Retrieved from http://www.bls.gov/news.release/empsit.t10.htm

Bureau of Labor Statistics. (2010). *Local Area Unemployment Statistics*. Retrieved from http://www.bls.gov/web/laumstrk.htm

Rosato, D. (2009, November 1). *The 50 Best Jobs in America*. Money. Vol. 38, Issue 11, p88. Retrieved from http://140.234.17.9:8080/EPSessionID=455884a7827a7946dcebcde6ab7704d/EPHost=proquest.umi.com/EPPath/pqdweb?index=0&did=1873255341&SrchMode=2&sid=1&Fmt=3&VInst=PROD&VType=PQD&RQT=309&VName=PQD&TS=1264493591&clientId=13118

Scholarship Hunter. (2010). *Government Scholarships and Grants for College*. Retrieved from http://www.scholarshiphunter.com/governmentcollegegrants.html

United States Department of Labor. (2010). *Unemployment Insurance*. Retrieved from http://workforcesecurity.doleta.gov/unemploy/

Employment Search Log				
Date	Company & Contact	Phone & Email	Type of Work	Remarks

Network Contacts				
Name	Title	Company	Phone# & Email	Remarks

NOTES:

About the Authors

Odie Smith is presently the customer service manager and regional manager with CBIZ Network Solutions, LLC in St. Louis, Missouri. He has simultaneously held these positions for the past 5 years. Mr. Smith has performed hundreds of interviews for technical and non-technical positions and has traveled to most major US cities performing job aptitude assessments and interviews. His discipline in professional decision making has granted him many company awards and honors, and he is nationally regarded as a customer service specialist. Mr. Smith has assisted many unemployed workers in the past eighteen years and will continue to provide his professional guidance. Mr. Smith's Business Administration degree and academic studies have prepared him for this direction.

Daval Smith is a certified pharmacy technician for a leading benefits management company in St. Louis, Missouri. She began her career through the St. Louis Community College system where she studied and excelled in child care development, which led her to pursue a career in the child care field. She worked several years as a youth instructor and helped to improve many young lives. In 1993, she and Mr. Smith established a non-profit company SmithCo, of which they distributed unemployment assistance information to workers in the St. Louis area who were casualties of layoffs. This experience led Mr. and Mrs. Smith to begin expanding their research and understanding of how to better serve those in need. Her leadership with assisting others has advanced her supportive direction to become an influence to co-produce *Mr. and Mrs. Smith's Employment Survival Guide.*

Currently, Mr. and Mrs. Smith are working on a series of family enrichment books. They have been happily married for twenty-two years, and they are raising their two teenage children, Odie Jr. and Aubrey.

www.ingramcontent.com/pod-product-compliance
Lightning Source LLC
Chambersburg PA
CBHW051449280526
45785CB00003B/1486